HUNTING
STARTER *KIT*
2-IN-1 BOXSET

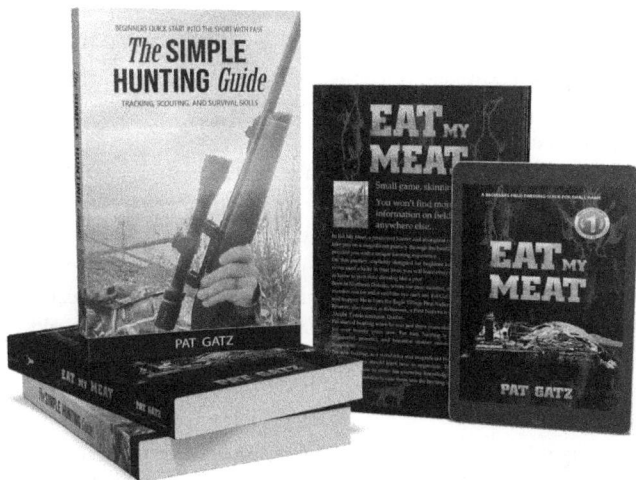

PAT GATZ

A Special Gift To Our Readers!

Included with your purchase of this book is our Field Dressing Starters Guide. This guide will prepare you with some essential critical tips not to forget when you start field dressing small game. It has a secret golden nugget at the end, too!

Click the link below and let us know which email address to deliver it to.

www.patgatz.com

CONTENTS

THE SIMPLE HUNTING GUIDE

CONTENTS

EAT MY MEAT

BEGINNERS QUICK START INTO THE SPORT WITH EASE

The SIMPLE HUNTING *Guide*

TRACKING, SCOUTING, AND SURVIVAL SKILLS

INTRODUCTION

No matter where we are in the world, we generally know where our food comes from. Fruits, vegetables, and meat (in all its varieties) come from farms before it arrives in the shops and lastly upon our plates. We are not truly in control of where our food comes from. Or are we? Some people go away for a few days a year and return with their freezers bursting with fresh meat. However, this meat wasn't simply picked up at a bulk sale. No, this meat was earned through dedication, hard work, and the ability to be patient. These people spend weeks gathering the necessary information, licenses, and equipment before traveling to get this meat. They earn it through hunting.

Why try hunting if your food can be bought at any corner store? It is simple. It isn't just about food. Yes, hunting is a way to replenish your meat stocks before winter, as well as a way for you to control where your food comes from, but it is so much more than just that. It's about getting out into nature and seeing what there is to see. It's a way to experience animals in their natural habitat and a way to protect them through conservation. A hunter doesn't go into the forest to kill. They go to harvest and make use of the animal they are looking for. A true hunter never wastes any animal, be it a squirrel, a fish, a rabbit, or even a moose. Hunting for the pot allows you to have a varied diet beyond what is simply available to you in a grocery store.

When you look at a hunter, you may expect to see a rugged, hardy person (with an excessive number of guns and knives) who is willing to do whatever they must to get their quarry. This leaves many people considering hunting, feeling that they can never live up to that standard that they believe a hunter should be. Yet, it is essential to note that no one is a standard hunter, and anyone can hunt. Yes, anyone can hunt. Whether you are an I.T. expert, a stay-at-home parent, or a CEO of a major company, you can hunt. Anyone can hunt. Even children who can pick up a slingshot can hunt small game. It is a simple practice but comes with great responsibility.

So, if you have found yourself sitting at your desk or home and aimlessly staring out into the distance wondering if you, yes you, can try your hand at hunting, know this: Yes, you can! With The Simple Hunting Guide: Beginners Quick Start Into The Sport With Ease - Tracking, Scouting, And Survival Skills, getting into hunting has never been simpler. This book aims to get you to start your first hunt with all the necessary information that you will ever need.

This essential hunter's guide contains everything from teaching you about the basics of hunter's education, firearm safety (if you will be using this kind of hunting tool), what kinds of prey are available to you, and the method. That means how you will harvest the animal, be it a bow, pellet gun, rifle, or even slingshot. See? You are already learning.

A hunter should always be prepared. You cannot just picture the result of your hunt because that is only the final step. You need to take several steps before setting foot into the location you will be hunting in. You will learn which tools are best suited for your particular hunt and what is needed to get the best from your outing.

However, what happens if something terrible happens? Prepare for the worst, and you will never be caught off guard. Learn about not only the animals you seek to harvest but also their predators. Start by practicing your skills on the smaller game before moving onto the larger animals. This will help you build confidence and sharpen your skills as you set your target on larger game. Each animal is different, and tracking them through their behavior and tracks is a vital skill to have, which this book offers.

By being fully prepared to enter the unknown, you will be able to tackle even the stickiest of situations where you may be forced to survive a few days out in the wilderness. I did say it's possible to become a hunter, not that it will be an easy feat. Hunting isn't just about loading a weapon and shooting the first animal you see. There is a lot to learn before you should even consider starting a hunt. Luckily, you have picked up the right book to help you through your beginner phase and become a veteran hunter.

Hunting is in everyone's blood, as this is how our ancestors lived before they settled and started to farm. We should all be able to return to the hunter-gatherer way if we are so inclined to. My name is Pat Gatz, and I am a native of Northern Ontario. This area is known for its dense forests and thick marshes for as far as the eye can see and even beyond that. This was where my wolf pack of siblings and I learned about respecting and gathering what we could from nature. As soon as I was old enough to hold a slingshot, I was hunting partridge, snakes, and any other animal that crossed my path. I was only three years old. There was no book out there to help me understand hunting and a collection of people who handed down their knowledge to make the best of my developing hunting skills.

I have been hunting for over 20 years. I have come to treat this activity not only as a sport but as a way for one to connect with nature, find inner peace, and find happiness while respecting the life around me. With so many years of hunting, I have found that it is time to hand down the knowledge presented to me as a youngster to the newer generation (new to hunting and not an age-related issue). My goal is to make sure that your very first hunt and sequential hunts after that go flawlessly, and you succeed in bagging your quarry time and time again.

Hunting is truly a primal skill that everyone will have a calling to at some point in their lives, and with this book at your side, you will be able to follow through with that call. Whether you hunt for the pot or trophies, may this book guide you with the knowledge that has taken me years to gather. Once you have completed this book, you will have an appreciation for hunting as a sport—one that is easy to get into once you are fully prepared. Dive into this hunting grail, a complete beginner's hunting know-how manual, to discover the joy of being out in the wilderness, stalking your prey while respecting it at the same time. There is simply no time like the present to pick up a new sport that will allow you the freedom that so many people long for; it will amass you fresh meat that will make your family and friends jealous at all the cookouts. Hunting is in your blood, so open this book and start your training to sharpen those dormant skills. Hunt to live, live to hunt!

CHAPTER 1

BASIC HUNTER EDUCATION

To improve at anything in life, you need to have a basic understanding and further education in that specific area. This holds very true to hunting. Before one can get a weapon to use in harvesting animals, you will need to understand what goes into hunting and how you can remain within the laws of your respective state/province. In the provinces of Canada and the states of America, there are vastly different laws involved in hunting and owning any kind of firearm. It is your responsibility to ensure that you know the laws of your respective area and where you will be hunting to ensure what documentation you may need to complete hunts in those areas. Since these areas are so vastly different, an overview of what to do and ask for will be presented in this chapter. When in doubt, it is a good idea to contact your state or province's specific—or the state/province you will be hunting in—Fish and Wildlife Service Department to get the answers to any of your questions.

HUNTER'S EDUCATION

Many places in America and Canada require that a person undergo an education course, known as Hunter Ed, before allowing them to get a license for hunting. This is an essential course for all those starting as the basics of hunting, gun safety, and various other aspects are covered to ensure that responsible hunters are going out into the world. Upon completing this kind of course, you will be presented with a National Hunter Education certificate and a Hunter Safety card that states that you have completed the course. This certificate should be accepted in any jurisdiction as long as the International Hunter Education Association—USA (IHEA-USA) requirements are met. This is called reciprocity and can also hold for various gun permits that may be needed. Before signing up and completing any Hunter Ed course, make sure that the IHEA-USA endorses them.

Hunter Ed is important in teaching you about gun safety and other safety tips to keep you safe when hunting in the wilderness. Other aspects of the course will include how to behave responsibly in nature. You are there to hunt, not poach. Know the hunting laws and the state/province laws to ensure that you conserve the natural environment, respect other hunters and the wildlife, and always make a clean kill. The course will also provide you with copious amounts of knowledge of applying yourself during a hunt and pointing out acceptable behavior while on a hunt. Lastly, the course also encourages that the new hunter becomes involved in hunting groups and conservation organizations. This means that you learn to work together with wardens and private landowners to preserve habitats and wildlife. Being a hunter isn't just about harvesting animals. It is also about managing wildlife and respecting the nature that you find yourself in.

The goal of Hunter Ed is to train safety-conscious, responsible, and law-abiding hunters. These courses are generally aimed at those new to hunting but make great refresher courses for those considered veteran hunters. By completing this course, you will promote responsible hunting behavior, become aware and abide by the different hunting laws and regulations, and lower the risk of hunting accidents while increasing your safety while you hunt.

If you find yourself wanting to hunt in a state/province that doesn't require a Hunter Ed certificate because of age or other factors, go ahead and complete it anyway. There is no downside to completing the course and so many benefits to having it, especially if you plan to use a firearm in your hunting. Hunter Ed can be completed online, in room, and field tested, so see for yourself which method you prefer and apply today! A Hunter Ed course can vary from free to upward of $30, so shop around for the course that best suits you, but ensure that it is compliant with all the regulations of the IHEA-USA (Krebs, 2020). Once you are certified, you never have to go through this course again unless you want to attend a refresher course. Remember to make copies of your card and certificate, and keep them in a safe place. It is also a good idea to keep your Hunter Ed number on your phone for safekeeping.

WEAPON LICENSES AND COURSES

Suppose you are planning to use firearms in your hunting travels. It is an excellent idea to make sure of the respective gun laws between the different states/provinces. What holds in one state/province may not be true in another, and you do not want to end up in hot water because of it. Although some states/provinces share reciprocity in terms of gun permits, this may not be true for others. Due to this, when you are traveling for hunting to a different state/province, you will need to ensure that you have the correct permits for your firearms or you may stand a chance of having them confiscated and being arrested!

It is strongly suggested that you take the time to become acquainted with the weapon you will be using to harvest on a hunt. There are many gun safety courses you can take to become certified in using a gun. (Tip: This is not always a requirement for getting your hunting license but a general safety suggestion.) Understanding and respecting a weapon makes it a valuable tool in the hands of the one handling it instead of a deadly implement that can have dire consequences when mishandled.

Although many states/provinces do not require you to have completed a bowhunter course, if you have completed Hunter Ed course, states like New York and Montana do. Due to this, always check before going on a hunt to avoid unnecessary fines.

General Firearm Safety Tips

Firearms are dangerous. They can and will kill, both intentionally and unintentionally. Understanding the safety involved with these hunting tools is what makes you not only an excellent hunter but one that will avoid harming themselves or others unintentionally. Here are some general tips that will help you with handling your hunting tool responsibly:

- Before making use of the weapon, ensure that the barrel is clean and clear of all obstructions.
- Use the correct ammunition with the weapon.
- Do not store the ammunition with the weapon.
- When the weapon is not in use, clear it of all ammunition.
- No running, climbing, or jumping with a loaded gun. There could be a misfire.
- No drinking of alcohol before or during a hunt.
- Only point the muzzle of a gun at its intended animal quarry and nothing else. Not even as a joke.
- Treat all guns as if they are loaded, period.
- Keep the safety on until you are ready to take a shot.
- Before firing at your target, be sure to know what is in front of it as well as behind it. Bullets can travel farther than most people think.
- Never rest your finger on the trigger. Keep it on the trigger guard until you are ready to take the shot.

Although many of these tips seem obvious for hunting when one is overconfident, you tend to forget the rules and make mistakes. If you are lucky, this kind of mistake will only cost you your quarry. If you are not, this will spell the end of your hunting adventure, one way or another.

LICENSE TO HUNT

You are now almost ready to get a license to hunt. Before you can get your license, you need to ask yourself what, when, where, and how. What are you going to hunt? Are you considering going after big game, predators, or small game? When will you go hunting? Some animals can only hunt at certain times of the year to avoid overhunting or possible pregnancies. You will need a general hunting license if you want to hunt these animals while in season. If for some reason you cannot hunt these animals within their hunting season, you will need to apply to get a special permit to hunt them outside of the allotted season. Where will you go hunting? Where you are from may not have the animal you wish to hunt. Research where this animal could be found and then get the necessary documentation ready to hunt that animal in its respective state/province. Keep in mind that some states like Colorado and California have a lottery system that awards hunting permits for certain large game, and there is no guarantee they will pick you. Some states and provinces will also be divided into different sections. You need to be sure that you are hunting in the correct area or fines may be possible.

How will you hunt? This is a crucial question you need to ask yourself. If you are not comfortable with firearms, there is no need to make use of them. There are several animals you can hunt with a bow during bow season. These include black bears, mule deer, and even elk. Keep in mind that rules determine what kind of bow or crossbow you are allowed to use during the different hunting seasons. If you prefer the smaller game, you can use snares, slingshots, or even pellet guns, as long as you are in season to do so and legal in the state or province. It is essential to look at what animal you will be hunting and the terrain you have access to. This will also help you determine which method of taking is best.

Now that you have answered all the questions, you can move along to getting your hunting license for the state/province you wish to hunt in. If you will be hunting with children or are not quite an adult yet, be aware of the age restrictions in the various states and provinces. If you are old enough to hunt, ensure that a parent gives consent to you doing so, as some states/provinces will not allow a minor to hunt without this. You will also need a valid form of identification to prove who you are. Be sure to have nothing against your name, such as outstanding fines or taxes, as this can prevent you from getting a license until it's paid in full. You may be asked to present your Hunter's Safety card as proof that you have completed Hunter Ed. Lastly, you will need to cover the costs associated with the license you wish to purchase. Each state/province will have its costs as well as different kinds of licenses that will be available. Some licenses only last for the hunting season, a year, or could be for a lifetime. Some licenses can even be extended or have days changed if you cannot make it for whatever reason. Contact the respective Fish and Game Department for that state/province to find out more about their various rules and regulations.

A website like Reserve America can help you get everything ready for the various hunting licenses you may need for the state or province you want to hunt, trap, or fish in. Once you have your license, you will be able to hunt most small game. However, suppose you are interested in a specific animal. In that case, you may need to purchase special tags or permits to go along with your hunting license. You can buy over-the-counter tags—which will allow you to hunt specific animals like deer or turkeys—or you can purchase draw tags. Draw tags are for high-demand animals but may not have the numbers to support the demand. There is a limited number of these tags, so it comes down to first come, first served, or a lottery system to see who is awarded these tags. If you prefer hunting migratory birds, you will have to purchase a yearly duck stamp that will allow you to do so.

OTHER PERMITS

If you want to hunt on public land, you will need to have a pass to access those lands. The most accessible pass covering most public areas where you may want to hunt is "America the Beautiful—The National Parks and Federal Recreational Lands Pass Series. Except for about 30 refuges with extra costs—such as entrance fees or parking fees—this pass allows a car of four individuals over the age of 16 entrance into most national parks. These passes help with the park's upkeep, covers your entrance fee, and allows for amenities to be maintained. Not all parks allow hunting, so make sure before you plan a hunt in your favorite hiking area!

This pass is renewable every year for about $80 for most people, while those in the military can pick it up for free. Seniors can get a lifetime pass for $80 or pay a yearly fee of $20. Those with a permanent disability—though this person doesn't have to be 100% disabled—can get the pass for free. Keep in mind that there may be extra costs involved in processing the ordering of this pass online. Still, it is worth having in the long run, especially if you are scoping the area for a possible hunt later in the season. What Can You Do Once You Have a License? Once you have your license, this doesn't mean that there aren't rules that you need to follow. Each state/province has its regulations and guidelines that you will need to follow or face various penalties. When hunting, only do so within the scope of the license you purchased. Don't hunt deer when you are not carrying a license to do so. Only hunt the approved animals at the correct place and time of the year. Follow the state/province requirements for the number of animals that can be harvested, as there are usually limits. If you are hunting big game, remember to tag your kills before dressing them for travel.

Failure to uphold these regulations could result in revoking your license for a limited period or permanently, fines, or even jail time. Follow what you were taught in Hunter Ed and be a conscientious hunter. Make sure that you stay up to date with all possible regulations every year.

If you find that you are not ready to fire a weapon, then consider going along on some hunts where you can learn from a mentor. It is from these people that you can pick up the tricks of the trade. They already know the animal's movements, what to look for when hunting certain animals, and how to avoid being spotted. You need to build up experience that doesn't always come from hunting yourself, so don't be afraid to look for a mentor to help you. Ensure that you have all the right equipment and be well versed in using all of it. If you haven't practiced using a gun, then you shouldn't be using it. Know what kind of clothing you should be wearing and if you need to be visible to other possible hunters.

WHERE MAY I HUNT?

Once you are fully licensed and have all other necessary documents ready, then the next thing you need to decide is what kind of land you will hunt on. There are only two possibilities: public or private. Regardless of which you hunt on, you will need to check the state or province's regulations to see if anything may be required on your part to hunt on these two lands.

If you aim to hunt on public land, you can do so as the state/province regulates hunting. There will be clear areas marked out for where you may and may not hunt, since everyone shares this land. This includes people who are hiking, camping, and bird watching. You will need to make sure that you get to know the land and come prepared with any equipment you may need on your hunts.

Public lands that are huntable include national wildlife refuges, Bureau of Land Management (BLM) managed public lands, as well as national preserves (U.S. Department of the Interior, 2017). As long as these are huntable lands and you have permission to be there, you may hunt for what your license allows you to.

Hunting on private land can become a little tricky as there are ever-changing laws—depending on which state or province you are in—surrounding this type of hunting. If a friend invites you to hunt on his property, you may not necessarily need a license. Still, a license is required if the property belongs to someone else. Not all states/provinces have public areas to hunt on, but there is an abundance of privately owned land that contains all manners of animals that may be hunted if the landowner allows it. This is where the rights of two specific types of people—landowners and hunters—have come under fire in recent years.

If a hunter stumbles onto land that has no post that states either "No Trespassing" or "No Entry," the consensus is that the property allows entrance for hunters to continue hunting. However, this land may be privately owned by an individual who may not want them hunting on their land. This has caused private landowners and hunters to butt heads several times in many years. Hunting is a deeply cultural aspect of many Americans' lives. With more and more land becoming privately owned, it is getting more difficult find places to hunt an individual who doesn't own that.

Don't feel disheartened by this, as there are many ways to get around this little hiccup. First, if you are planning to hunt in an area that may see you going onto private property, all you need to do is to find out if it is posted or not. If the property is posted—where a warning has been placed to say no trespassing or hunting is allowed—you can simply ask the owner for permission to have access to the land. It is generally good manners to do this several days before your hunt happens and not do it while hunting. Unless the owner has a sanctuary on their property or they don't want animals killed there, there is a good chance that you may be allowed to hunt on the property. Some owners may even strike a deal with you where you can pay to hunt on their property or they may want a share of your harvest. However, if an owner says no, you do not have access to the land and can be arrested for trespassing if caught on the property. Be sure to get confirmation of permission in writing just to be sure.

If an owner has refused your entrance to his property, there are only two reasons that you may go onto their land. The first is that you have wounded prey that has crossed the border or your hunting dogs have run onto the property. You must make sure both are retrieved and contact the owner to make them aware of your intent and reason for being on their property.

If privately owned land has been correctly posted, it will be clear for all to see. Each state/province has its own set of rules for how posting should be done, but the general rule for you as a hunter is to look out for several things. The first is several signs that state no entry. These can generally be found at vehicle entrances, corners of the property, and sometimes spaced out along a fence every quarter mile or so. These signs need to be legible and visible to any who may stumble across them. These signs may also be painted in bright colors such as orange or yellow to draw attention.

Sometimes the posting is not obvious, so if you are hunting and come across livestock, buildings, or cultivated land, you are in an area that you should not be. An owner may even ask you to leave, in which case it is something you need to do whether the land is posted or not. As a hunter, you need to make sure you do not enter private property. If you see a posting and ignore it, you are now hunting illegally and are, therefore, a poacher. If caught, you will lose your hunting license.

The postings are not only for your benefit but also for those on the property. Suppose the landowner is aware that there is a hunter on his land. In that case, he is likely to ensure that his livestock isn't in an area where they can get shot and ensure that other people on his property are wearing bright clothes that prevent accidental or fatal shootings. Even traps left by poachers are dangerous to the landowner, people, or animals of the property.

Luckily, many states/provinces are approaching private landowners to convince them to allow hunters onto their land. These states/provinces generally help cover possible losses or damages that may be sustained due to negligent hunters or aid the owner with extra labor or monetary rewards. Hunting is, after all, a national pastime and should be protected as much as possible. Be a responsible hunter: Ask permission to be in a privately owned place, and never enter a property where you have been denied access.

CHAPTER 2

PRACTICAL SURVIVAL EQUIPMENT AND GEAR

Now that all the paperwork has been obtained, it is time to make sure your gear and attire are ready. It isn't as simple as falling into a camping store and getting everything in one go. It will take time and some research to find the brands and items that you may prefer over another. Use the following information to do your research on what you may need personally when hunting, as some tools may not suit the type of hunt you are planning. Once you have an idea of what is perfect for you, put a shopping list together and get what is on it. Then, when you are ready to get everything gathered for your hunt—a few days before departing—have a checklist prepared to make sure that you do not forget anything. Preparation for a hunt is what takes the longest time, so spend some time setting up an appropriate checklist not to forget anything. Remember, there are no stores out in the wilderness. Once you are there and find yourself in need of something, you will have to make do without or develop creative ways to get around the problem.

HUNTING GEAR

You can get several items for yourself, but you have to decide what kind of hunt you will be going on before you get distracted by all the nifty tools. Knowing what sort of hunt you want to be a part of will determine what tools you will need. You will have no use for a pelvis saw if you are hunting rabbits. For the sake of this book, it is the smaller game animals that will be concentrated on, and even then, various tools are needed for different animals.

The first necessary thing is a decent backpack that is suited for your frame and strength. It needs to be not only sturdy enough to carry everything you may need but also manageable. You will be hiking for some distance after your quarry, so if your pack is too heavy when you start, imagine how heavy it will be when you come back with any potential prizes. The size of the backpack is determined by how long you want to be out hunting, so be sure to pack responsibly.

A skill you may need to brush up on is reading a map and using a compass. You can plan your hunting route on a map and become familiar with possible landmarks as a way to encourage yourself to not only rely on a global positioning system (GPS). This is not to say that you cannot use a GPS, but you will need to have a backup if the system fails. If you plan to use a GPS, then ensure that you have tested it well before going on your trip. Make sure the batteries it uses are fully charged, and you have spares for it. You can even make use of power banks to aid you in this. However, keep in mind that all of this does add to the weight you will have to carry with you. Many places where you can hunt may not have a decent signal, so ensure that the maps you are planning on using can be used in airplane or offline mode. OnX is one of the GPS map apps that many hunters and wardens trust to get around while searching for their specific quarry. Be responsible for plotting where you are going and informing people of when you are leaving, where you are going, and for how long. These three important aspects can mean the difference between finding you if you get lost or remaining lost in the wilderness forever.

Other possible electronics that you can make use of are handheld torches or headlamps. Although a headlamp allows your hands to be free if you are moving around or carrying something, both are great tools to have. If you are hunting in a group—with a mentor or friends—you can also use two-way radios for communication. Ensure that you have the correct batteries for all the electronics you are carrying or all the wires necessary for charging the items from power banks. If you are hunting in a group and want to scout ahead, make sure that you have some kind of trail-marking tape to mark your route to find your way back or others can find you. There is nothing quite as scary as getting lost. If this happens to you—and this is possible— the first thing you have to do is not panic. The rest of the survival tips will be covered in Chapter 3.

When one is hunting for prey, you will primarily be using your eyes. You can pick up where an animal has gone by disturbed brush, fur left on trees, or tracks and scat, but sometimes, you may want to look a little further than what is just under your nose. A good set of binoculars will help you look for prey either in the sky, trees, or among the brush. Do not skimp on quality binoculars. Some animals are easier to hunt when you use a specific call to attract them. If you know what animal you are after, and you know the call they make, then you can make use of animal calls or even prerecorded sounds to take with you. This is not a must for all animals, so make sure your quarry needs this before just taking it along.

You will need a knife and a good one at that. Whether you find yourself having to dress your kill or defend yourself in the wilderness, a knife is essential. You can choose many knives, with some people preferring to use either fixed blades, folding knives, or the ever-popular multi-tool, which has several other functions. Each of these has its pros and cons, but it is up to your preference in deciding which is best to use. Regardless of what knife you are planning on using, make sure that you have a tool that can sharpen it. There is nothing more frustrating than having a dulled tool and not doing what it must to make your life easier.

Whether you are thinking of making a single-day trip or several, it is a good idea to take some sort of shelter with you. You may think it is unnecessary, but if the weather suddenly turns nasty, you will have one more tool in your arsenal that will protect you. Something as simple as a space blanket or bivy sack can keep you warm and safe until such time that the weather improves and you can keep moving. For longer days in the wilderness, you can consider other shelter methods or ways to sleep, which can even include hammocks. These shelters should be heavily dependent on the season you are hunting in, so make sure to have the appropriate equipment that goes with the season. Other items you may need if you are going to be out for a few days are cooking utensils to cook and enjoy warm meals. These can also be used to help gather water when necessary.

Paracord (parachute cord) is a must-have item whether you are hiking or hunting. From replacing a snapped boot-lace to a damaged bag cord to even hoisting your food up into a tree, this item has multiple functions and should be in all hunting bags. However, it is available in many stores in various lengths; however, check the breaking strength to determine the kind of function it will have to fulfill.

Other items that could come in handy but are dependent on the animal you are hunting are blinds and decoys. Some animals will only come close to you if they see others like themselves. If you are going to make use of blinds, be sure to sit still and comfortably. Get a few cushions, but don't fall asleep.

HUNTING ATTIRE

You need to make sure that what you wear is comfortable, protective, keeps you hidden, and makes sure that you can be seen. Many people assume that you will need to wear camouflage clothes so that the animals do not see you, but this is not true for all states/provinces. Some state and province regulations insist that you wear a high visibility vest and cap—usually orange in color—when hunting. This is to prevent other hunters from accidentally shooting you as you move through the wilderness.

Depending on the season you are hunting in, you may require extra layers of clothing to protect you from the cold or rain. The inner layer (or base layer) is there to not only keep you warm but also to keep moisture away from your skin. Hunting is hard work, and you will sweat. There is nothing worse than wet socks and underwear as you are walking, so because of this, the base layer needs to be made of a synthetic material (such as polyester) which creates a wicking effect that draws water away from your skin. Although cotton seems warmer, it absorbs moisture and keeps it close to the skin, which in turn will develop hot spots and blisters if you remain in those wet clothing items.

The outer layer—such as jackets or rainwear—needs to be waterproof and puncture proof. This layer will protect you from the elements and needs to be of high-quality material. The orange vest, if you need to wear one, will go over this. Depending on what animal you are hunting for, you can make use of scent-reduced clothing. Gloves and socks need to have a wicking effect and stand a good chance of getting wet if you are moving through the brush. Consider having a few sets of dry, clean socks in your pack, as this is how you will prevent blisters from developing. When the biting insects get to be too much, you can use bug netting draped over your hat to keep them out of your face if you do not want to use insect repellent.

The most important piece of clothing you will need is a good set of worn-in boots. These are what will protect your feet and make walking vast distances bearable. Never go hunting or hiking with a new pair of boots. The blisters will drive you insane. Boots worn during the spring and summer should be the same size as your everyday shoes. In contrast, those worn in the fall and winter need to be up to a size larger to accommodate the thicker socks you will need to make use of.

VITAL EXTRAS

These tools are not limited to hunting but rather of importance to anyone who plans on going out into the wilderness. The most vital is a basic first aid kit. This is only a starter kit, though. You will need to ensure that you know how to use everything in this kit and adapt it to one that can cover all the potential problems that can occur during a hunt. A standard first aid kit purchased from a pharmacy may not have everything that is required. The longer you are out hunting, the more items you need to have in your first aid kit. There are some no-compromise necessities such as gauze pads, butterfly bandages, Band-Aids, alcohol wipes, moleskin (for blisters), tweezers, antibiotic cream, allergy ointment, antihistamine of choice, an EpiPen, if required, ibuprofen (or painkiller of choice), surgical gloves (an allergy-free type), duct tape (a lot of this), SAM splint (flexible splint), anti-diarrhea medication, a Sharpie marker, and medical tape. Duct tape can take up a lot of space, so don't hesitate to wrap it around other items such as pencils, Sharpies, or even lighters to save space. If you have any personal or chronic medication, you will also need to pack this into your kit.

For a more advanced first aid kit, consider adding the following to help with more severe wounds that can occur. A hemostatic agent (such as QuikClot) to help stop the bleeding or make it more manageable until more fully trained help can arrive. Only if you have been trained to do so can you make use of a suture kit. If you have not been trained to do so, manage the wound with Steri-Strips or butterfly bandages. You can make use of liquid stitches or super glue to manage cuts that are not too serious. Pressure dressings not only apply pressure to a wound but also keep the dressings in place. Due to this, infection is limited, and it can stem the flow of blood. Ensure that you have enough gauze rolls, tape, dressing, and cohesive wrap so that you can manage wounds that may need redressing. If you are not using a water purifier or packing enough clean water, consider purchasing some water treatment tablets. Unpurified water can bring nasty stomach issues that can leave you dehydrated and too weak, so always stick to drinking clean water. Dehydration can be easily combated with some electrolytes in either a powdered form or a fizzy tablet. These can also provide energy to help you get through some of the difficult hikes you may have to do when looking for your quarry.

A first aid kit is only as good as what you put into it. Make sure you have quality items that have not expired. Go through the contents every couple of months to ensure that everything is up to standard. Taking an introductory first aid course isn't necessary. Still, it is something that will come in handy if a disaster were to strike. Consider doing this if for no reason other than to be fully prepared.

Sunblock is necessary, even in the middle of winter, so be sure to make use of it. You can even get lip balms containing sun protection (SPF), which can protect your lips from getting sunburned. However, it isn't just the sun that you will need to protect yourself. Whining and biting insects are a bane to all who want to enjoy a pleasant hunt.

Insect repellents in the form of sprays, wipes, or ointments will protect you from their irritating bites. However, if you are concerned that this smell may cause your quarry to avoid you, you will need to ensure that the clothes you wear can cover all the areas prone to bites.

You can never assume that all your hunts will be successful, so it is crucial to pack food and water. You can use several foods, such as jerky, gummy sweets, or even prepared food such as boiled eggs and sandwiches. You can even learn to make your own pemmican (a trail food consisting of fat and powdered meat) or trail mix to help you with the energy required for a hunt. Foods that you take with you should contain about 40% carbohydrates, 30% fat, and 30% protein to cover all your body's needs. Although food and water go hand in hand, water is most vital to your survival. You can quickly get dehydrated in a matter of hours and be dead in three days if you do not have access to water. You can carry water with you, or you will need to have a purification system.

Other miscellaneous items that will benefit you is dental floss (with a sturdy needle to fix any possible tears), black bags (excellent ground cover as well as a way to get rid of your trash), a foldable shovel (to dig pit latrines if needed), toilet paper, a fire-making kit (can include matches, lighters, and flints), zip ties, game bags, fishing kit (if your license allows for fishing, or at the very least some fishing line), writing equipment (pen, pencil, and writing pad), snare wire (or picture hanger wire), and a set of dry towels.

POSSIBLE HUNTING WEAPONS

As a hunter, you are spoiled for choice when it comes to what and how you hunt. There are many small game options which can be seen in the table below. Each animal has several ways in which you can hunt them.

Small mammals	Rabbits and hares: snowshoe hare, cottontail, and jackrabbit. Squirrels: red, gray, and fox squirrels. Prairie dogs, marmots, groundhogs, and woodchucks. Foxes (furbearers or predators): gray, red, and swift foxes. Furbearers: beavers and muskrats. Furbearers or predators: weasels, ferrets, martens, fishers, wolverines, mink, badgers, and skunks. Predators: Bobcats, lynx, and coyotes.
Birds	Grouse (upland birds): sage grouse, sharp-tailed, ruffed, blue, and Franklin's. Doves (upland birds): mourning dove, pigeon, squab (young pigeon), or rock dove. Quail (upland birds): bobwhite, scaled quail, mountain, California, and Gambel's. Partridge (upland birds): gray and chukar partridge. Pheasants (upland bird). Woodcocks and Snipe (upland birds). Turkey (upland bird). Geese (waterfowl): Canadian, Brant geese, and snow. Ducks (waterfowl): mallard, pintail, American black, wood, teal, ruddy duck, and canvasback. Swans (waterfowl): tundra, trumpeter, tundra, black, and black-necked swan. Cranes (waterfowl): sandhill crane.

| Reptiles & Amphibians | Frogs: American toad, Fowler's toad, bullfrog, northern gray treefrog, northern spring peeper, western chorus frog, and northern cricket frog. |
| | Turtle: snapping turtles. |

Not all areas allow for snares and traps, so be sure to check regulations before deciding on using these hunting methods.

Snares and Traps

These hunting methods can be used by a hunter who wishes to keep the pelts in good condition or simply try to survive because something went wrong and they have no other option. There are several types of snares that you can make use of to catch smaller animals. These include the simple snare (placed in the middle of an animal run or over its burrow) and a twitch snare (a simple snare attached to a sapling that catches the animal and pulls it into the air). The snare has a clinch system that tightens as the animal struggles. Simple snares can be added to a squirrel pole, which squirrels use to run up into trees to catch various animals such as squirrels and martens. You can use either snare wire or picture hanging wire to make these snares.

Traps like the deadfall trap use a heavy object (usually a rock) held up with sticks and bait under it. The prey item—usually a rat, mouse, or another type of rodent—will come for the bait and disturb the trap, which will cause the rock to land on them.

CUT NOTCH

CUT NOTCH AND BIND
TOP PART AWAY TO
CREATE SLIGHT CRACK
UP THE STICK

BEND AT NOTCH

BEND AT TOP
OF CRACK

BEND INTO THE H4
CARVE NOTCH AND
HOLDING EDGE

DEAD-FALL
2 STACKED ROCKS

If you are looking to catch bait for fishing, you can use the bottle fish trap. When looking at a two-liter plastic soda bottle, you remove the first quarter of it—which includes the neck—and you invert it into the remaining part of the bottle. Alternatively, you can use two bottles where the head and neck section is pushed into another bottle with only a small portion of the bottom removed. Ensure that the two pieces are held together by something that can be removed later. Add to a stream, tie it in place, and wait. Small bait fish will swim into the trap but will find themselves unable to swim out again.

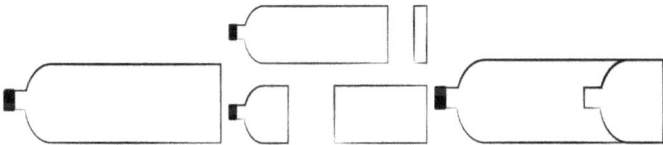

(Tip: If using two bottles, ensure that the cap at the end of the trap is in place or the fish will just swim straight out.)

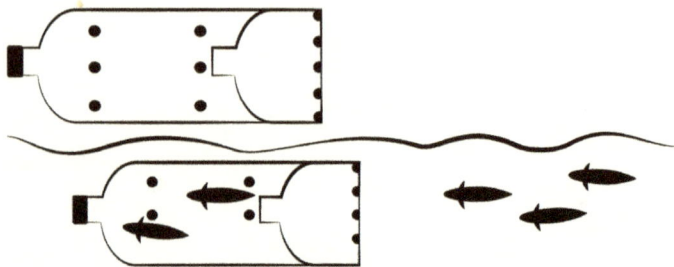

(Tip: When making use of these hunting methods, you must check the traps regularly. Not only to collect what you catch but also to dispatch any animal humanely or to prevent any predator from making off with a meal source that may be vital for your survival.)

Slingshots

Although not legal in several states/provinces, this tool can be made or bought—depending on your preference—and can be used to hunt several small game animals or varmints. Treat a slingshot the same way you would a gun, as it too can cause considerable damage in an untrained hand. Make sure to have eye protection to ensure your safety. Th e key to making a slingshot work in your favor is two things: the correct ammo and the correct prey.

When looking at potential ammo, do not use something that can break upon impact and cause shards to ricochet straight back at you. Using ball bearings or smooth stones is your best bet in place of marbles. Th e animals you can stalk with a sling include rabbits, pheasants, wild turkeys, other fowl, squirrels, ducks, and pigeons. It is key that you get within a short range so that you get a headshot off . One shot, one kill! Th e key to hunting is to ensure you kill humanely. As you will need to get close to your chosen prey, you will need to learn how to stalk, so make sure that your chosen ammo doesn't make any sounds while you move around, alerting your potential prey to your whereabouts.

Making a Slingshot

Making your slingshot is as easy as going outside and looking for the right branch. You are looking for a forked branch (Y-shaped) where each of the forks is roughly the same diameter. Cut the slingshot to your preferred size using a saw. If you are not in a survival situation, you can dry your branch using the microwave. Before you do this, ensure that you have weighed the wood, as this will be your indication of moisture loss. Do not take off the bark, as this could cause the wood to crack. Microwave the wood at one-minute intervals while flipping the piece of wood each time to ensure equal water loss. Th e wood should be losing weight per minute. Depending on what kind of tree you cut this from will determine the moisture content. Th e drying process is complete when the piece of wood no longer loses weight.

Watch this process closely as you do not want the wood to start charring or smoking. Once dry, cut notches about half an inch from the top of each of the forks, making sure they are the same length on each fork. You will need to get

some power bands that can be store-bought ones for slingshots, or you can use the inner tube of a tire. Make sure the
lengths are the same.

Next, lash the one open end of the powerband to the
one notch using string or dental floss. You can make use of
the constrictor knot or any other knot that prevents slippage.
Repeat for the other fork. Take a piece of leather or other
strong material that is handy, and fashion the pouch that
your ammo will rest in. Make two slits in the material as
you will need to attach the power bands.

Push the power bands through the slits and tie them
back onto themselves with a knot that will not slip or unravel through use.

Now you have a working slingshot that will not warp as you use it because you have dried it. Try to avoid air drying, as this can cause the wood to crack, especially if you have removed the bark beforehand.

Pellet Guns

These types of guns are a step before true firearms which are just as deadly, so treat them as if they were the real thing. These weapons shoot metallic projectiles that can either be metal ball bearings (B.B.) or non-spherical pellets. Unlike firearms powered by gunpowder, these weapons can be powered by compressed CO_2 (carbon dioxide), a pump, pre-charged pneumatic (PCP), or spring charged.

This is a lightweight, easy-to-use weapon that is more accurate than most B.B. guns over a longer distance. It is also a quiet weapon, so you may have a second chance to hit your target if, for some reason, you missed the first time.

There are a variety of makes and models for pellet guns. However, suppose you are planning on hunting with this weapon. In that case, it is a good idea to use the rifle variety over the handgun type. This weapon can be used to hunt animals such as rabbits, birds, squirrels, and mice.

Not only should these weapons be treated with the same reverence as a powerful firearm but it also needs to be cleaned like one. The barrel needs to be cleaned after a hunt and obstructions removed when a misfire happens. Teach yourself how to take your weapon apart, clean it, and put it back together. If you treat your tools with respect, they will always be in top working order. Also, consider wearing eye protection when using pellet guns due to possible ricochets.

.410 Bore

This is the smallest caliber of the shotguns you can make use of for hunting. With next to no kick and cheap to reload, if you want to learn to shoot with a shotgun, this a great place to start. It is a good weapon at close range (25 yards). However, there isn't much shot per shell, so this does limit you on what you can hunt.

Some people say they have hunted many animals with this weapon. It is generally the kind of tool that is used for hunting turkeys. This shotgun is perfect for someone who is of a smaller size or very young. You may need to use a larger gauge shotgun to hunt animals such as rabbits, doves, or other game birds. That is not to say that you can't use this weapon, but rather that you will need to learn how to stalk your prey and take shots from a significantly closer range than most other firearms.

.22 Long Rifle (.22 LR)

This is an excellent firearm that doesn't have much recoil, noise, or even muzzle flash. It is a reliable tool that is light-weight enough to use while crossing long distances after prey. It is easy to fire either from a standing or prone position. Although this weapon shoots a smaller round than most other hunting weapons, it can be just as powerful and accurate in the right hands.

Unlike most hunting ammunition, the .22 is a rimfire which makes for cheaper ammunition. Still, you will not reload the ammunition as you would with most of the centerfire ammunition. However, at a fifth of the price of most 9mm rounds, it is worth it. The .22 LR comes in a variety of forms such as bolt action, pump action, semi-automatic, as well as lever action, so you can shop around for which you prefer to use. This well-rounded weapon is used for small game hunting, varmint control, target shooting, and survival.

As rimfire ammunition tends to be smaller than center-fire ammunition, there is less damage to the meat of your prey when it is shot. There are many animals you can hunt with this type of weapon. This includes smaller animals such as rabbits, squirrels, prairie dogs, and larger animals such as small deer, foxes, and wild hogs. The larger animals must be shot within a short to medium range (20–50 meters/21–54 yards), and always aim for the head or neck to ensure a quick, clean kill.

Regardless of what and where you are hunting, the only way to ensure that your trip is a success is to make sure that you are as fully prepared as possible. Expecting the worst and being prepared for it means you can handle whatever situation can be thrown at you. This chapter is but a guide. It is strongly suggested that you continue to do your research and prepare yourself fully.

CHAPTER 3

HOW TO SURVIVE—WHAT EVERY HUNTER MUST KNOW

Having the tools ready for an emergency is one thing, but knowing how to use them correctly can mean the difference between a few miserable days in the wilderness while help is on the way or something far worse. You are out there alone—or maybe with a couple of people; if something goes wrong and help is too far away, you will need to know how to protect yourself and anyone with you. Although there are several ways you can try to prepare yourself—such as checking the weather, going on first aid courses, and so on—sometimes something unexpected can occur. It is during this time that a true hunter will rise to the challenge.

GETTING LOST

When leaving civilization, there is always a chance that you can get lost. There are no roads or signs the farther you travel into the wilderness. This is why you must be familiar with the land you are traveling to, having both scoped it on a map as well as your GPS. However, even the best-laid plans can go awry. You can miss the path, slip and fall, miss a turn, and now you are hopelessly lost. The first thing you need to do is not to panic. Getting lost can be seen as a badge of honor and may have to be overcome sooner than later. When was the last time you checked your map? Can you backtrack? If so, go ahead and do this for a few minutes. If after 10 minutes nothing seems familiar, then stop and reassess the situation.

If you have some kind of communication device with a signal, then use it to call for help with the exact coordinates from your GPS. Rather, be a little embarrassed at having to be rescued than spending a night out in the wilderness. If you are with a group of people, simply calling them to alert them about where you are is the best thing you can do. This may chase your prey away, but it will ensure that you are found. You can continue to do this every couple of minutes. If, after 10 minutes, no one has come to your rescue, then your survival is up to you. Remember that well packed backpack of yours? Well, it is what will keep you safe until such time that you can be rescued. Don't be brave and tough it out trying to walk in a random direction because you are sure civilization is in that direction. Instead, take the time to prepare several lifesaving methods—especially if the weather has turned bad—instead of losing that time and end up being more lost and unprepared.

NOW WHAT?

The first thing that you will need to do is to fight your feelings. Being lost in the wilderness is not something we are prepared for in life. Imagination can be both a wonderful and deadly thing when you are in this mindset. Some people may imagine that this is where they die while others start to hatch a plan. This is what separates a true survivor from someone that may not make it. You came prepared for this possibility, so you only need to sit and think about how you will survive. Take stock of what kinds of resources are at your disposal in your immediate vicinity, as well as what remains in your pack. Do not go wandering farther from your current situation! If you got injured while getting lost, now is a good time to go over your injuries and treat them as best as possible. Once you have assessed that you can still move around, now is the time to build a shelter.

Shelter

A human can last up to three days without water. Still, he can die within a few hours due to hyperthermia (overheating) or hypothermia (too cold). You either need to get warm or cool down as quickly as possible. The shelter doesn't need to be a log cabin. Keep it small and easy to insulate if the weather is cold, or open and ventilated if hot. Even if you have a bivy sack or a space blanket, a simple shelter is enough to keep most of the elements at bay and points to the fact that a human is in the vicinity. This will help other people to find you.

Regardless of whether you are building a simple or a fully protected shelter, you will need to start with a sturdy frame, or you may find that the structure meant to keep you safe collapses around you. When in a forest, see if you can spot two saplings or small trees about six to seven feet apart. If this isn't something you see around you, but there are sparse trees, you can cut down a sapling then bring it closer to another tree. Dig a 12-inch hole to bury this sapling. These two standing trees or saplings will be the start of your frame. Find another sapling or thick branch that you can tie vertically between these two standing saplings—this will be your weight-bearing support beam—and tie it at the height of choice. Tie it higher for cooling down and lower for insulating your heat. Alternatively, suppose a tree nearby has some low-hanging branches that are sturdy. In that case, you can stake one into the ground, and it can be both the support beam and secondary part of the frame.

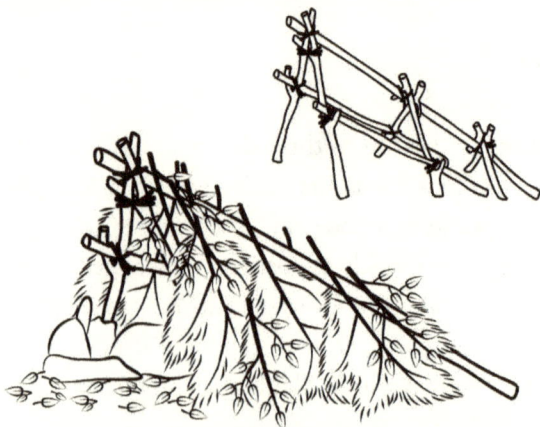

Ensure that your support beam isn't rotten and can take some weight. Once the frame is sturdy, you can add up to five layers of thick branches angled from the ground to your support beam. By placing these branches at an angle, it will help with keeping the rain off of you. You can use longer branches for a shelter against heat and shorter for a refuge against the cold. Cut these branches from trees where necessary and ensure that no insects or animals can bite you while you work. Depending on the situation you find yourself in, you can decide to build two walls—which can give the appearance of a tent—or a single wall which is the traditional shelter. Continue to pack on these branches until the entire length of your shelter is covered.

Once the angled roof is complete, the next step is to start waterproofing and insulating it. Collect small branches with leaves and pack them along the wall, first running horizontally and vertically until the layer is about a foot thick. If you still find gaps, you can fill those with more leaves, smaller sticks, bark, moss, and even pine needles. If you sit or lie in the shelter, you should not see outside through the wall. Now you know that it is truly well insulated.

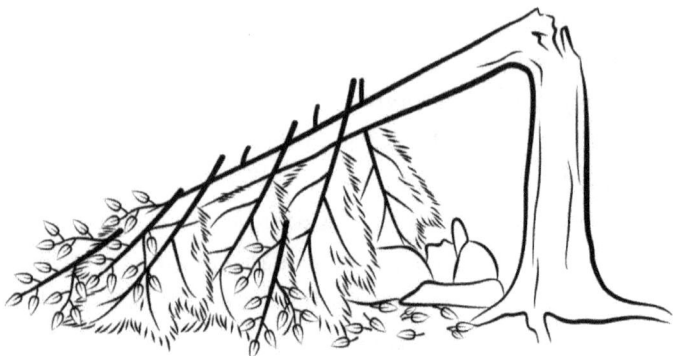

The next step is the floor of your shelter. Suppose you are trying to protect yourself from the heat. In that case, you need to clear the spot of debris and dig down into the ground, which will be significantly cooler than the air around you. Keep yourself from dehydrating and wait to do anything further until it is cooler not to waste any of your precious water. Suppose you need to protect yourself from the cold. In that case, you will also have to clear the area of debris before laying down an insulating layer, as the ground will be cold.

The same material you used to insulate your shelter's walls is good enough for your ground cover. If you have a groundsheet or black bags, you can lay this down over the insulating layer to give you more protection. You can even cover the entrance with this insulating material to keep the warmth in your small shelter.

(Tip: There are several ways to build a shelter—as is seen in the images. Which one you decide to build comes down to the materials that you find in your proximity and equipment you have with you.)

Water

Once your shelter is complete, you need to work on finding a fresh source of clean water to keep you going. If there is a storm or it is too hot, it is best to remain in your shelter and do what you have until the dangerous weather has passed. Once it is safe to do so, you can scope the area around you to find moving water. Ensure that you are marking your trail, as you do not want to get separated from your only shelter. If you cannot locate fresh, moving nearby water, look around you to see if there are any catchment areas where water may pool naturally. This water is likely stagnant, but it is worth collecting and storing until such time that you can boil it to make it safe. If there is snow nearby, you can collect that, but do not eat the snow directly! It takes a lot of energy to warm your body, and you will just lower it to the point of hypothermia if you are going to eat snow constantly. Instead, collect it and melt it down.

If you are uninjured, you can also dig for water. Look for plants known to grow close to water sources, such as cattails, willows, or cottonwood (Dumbauld, 2019). Dig a hole close to this plant until you notice moisture in the soil. Dig a little deeper and widen the hole. You have just created a weep hole that will naturally collect the water rising from the ground.

You can also collect water from plants directly because of the dew that lands on them. Be careful when taking water from plants directly without knowing what kind of plant it is. Some plants contain toxic components that can make your bad situation even worse. Only drink from plants that you recognize as safe. You can also tie plastic bags—such as Ziploc bags—around clusters of leaves, as when the plant goes through its respiration cycle, a by-product is water. Lastly, you can simply leave a piece of cloth or towel out to collect dew which can then be squeezed out and collected. Always ensure that you have some sort of container with you when hunting to collect water in it.

Many of these water-catching techniques are not quick. They will take some time to give you more than just a few mouthfuls of this lifesaving liquid, so be sure to have as many different types of catchments and learn to ration as much as possible without getting dehydrated.

Fire

You can never assume that the water you collect is clean, so it is always a good idea to boil it for a few minutes to get rid of any kind of pathogens that can lead to an upset stomach. Fire is essential not only because it can keep your water supply clean, but it can also keep you warm, cook any meals you manage to catch, and protect you from possible predators. A warm, full belly makes any situation a lot easier to deal with.

Starting a fire may be simple enough, but keeping it alive and going is something that takes a little more preparation and planning. You should already have the tools to help you create the fire, so move to the preparation for what else you may need. The success of any fire is keeping it fueled from birth until your rescue, so set out to find tinder, kindling, and fuelwood (thick sticks or branches). If you have a fire starting kit in your pack, there may already be tinder ready for you to use, but if not, create your own by collecting dried leaves, grass, finger-length twigs, or even pine needles. These items need to be dry to catch fire. Collect enough to create a bundle that can be held between your two hands with fingers touching. Next, collect some kindling. Kindling can be small sticks that should be no thicker than your index finger. You will need to collect about a generous armful. After that, it is time to look for fuelwood. This wood is about the thickness of your wrist, the length of your arm, and you need to collect enough that the stack comes to just under your knee.

Once everything has been collected, you can also look for some stones to help protect your fire and create a firepit. Whether you are trying to survive or not, this is not the time to forget that it is very dangerous when a fire isn't controlled. You need to clear debris away from where you want to build your fire. The distance from your shelter to your fire will be determined by the type of weather you are exposed to. Once the debris has been removed, you can dig down a little into the ground to create your firepit. Stones can also surround this firepit to help protect it from the wind while trying to light the tinder.

Build a small teepee with your kindling in the firepit first. Then take your tinder and create a nest into which you add a lit match, light a tinder bundle with a lighter, or make some scrapings from a magnesium block and lighting it with a striker. Add the lit tinder to the teepee of kindling and gently blow on the bundle until the flame starts to consume it and starts on the kindling. Continue to add more kindling until the fire begins to grow in strength. Once the kindling pile starts to diminish, then add the fuelwood around it. You can stack it around the fire or create another teepee over it. Now you have a fire.

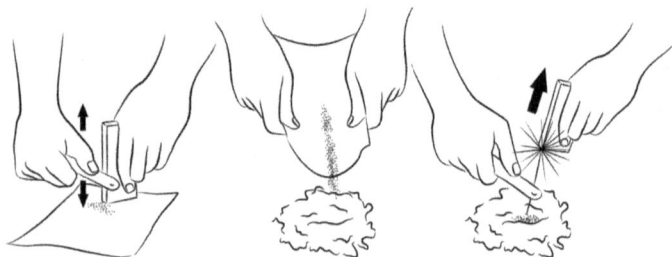

(Tip: Do not breathe in close to the smoking tinder as you will get
a lung full of smoke that is dangerous. Breathe away from it, then
gently blow out over it.)

If it is freezing, you can add stones to the fi re, allowing
them to heat up before burying them under a layer of dirt
and insulation at the bottom of your shelter to help you remain warm during the night. This is a surefire way to create
smokeless heat within your shelter. Be careful not to burn
yourself while trying this. Aim to pick up the hot rocks with
a Y-shaped stick so that you do not touch them directly.

What happens if you lose your fire-making equipment?
Well, then you need to learn how to make a bow drill. As
long as you have a knife or multi-tool, paracord or rope,
and wood, you can make this ancient tool to give you fire.
You will need a flat piece of medium to hard type wood
(this will be your fireboard or hearth board) with a socket
in it—you can cut it into the wood—and a spindle made
of the same wood. The fire board should be between 1 to
2 inch thick and at least twice as wide as your spindle. The

spindle needs to be made with a straight piece of wood with a diameter of half of an inch with a length of about 8-12 inches, preferably round in shape. The top end must taper off to a blunted point, while the bottom should also taper but not as sharply. This will go into the fireboard. These two pieces of wood must be dry!

Next, you will need to make your handhold and you bow. The handhold will be placed on top of the spindle to hold it in place, creating a notch for where this point will be, and bore some wood out. You will need to grease this area, as you do not want it to smoke while making an ember. The bow needs to be about the length of your forearm, slightly curved, and have a little flexibility to it. You will tie the paracord to both ends to create a bow with little slack in the cord. Take the spindle, ensuring that it has no bark still attached to it, and set it against the cord, making sure that it is in the center of the spindle. Twist the top of the spindle to the bottom, wrapping the cord around it. The cord should loop around the spindle—keeping it in place—with the bow on one side. Th e spindle should be on the outer edge of the cord and not between it and the bow. Do not let the cord rub against itself. Th e best way to achieve this is to angle the bow slightly downward when you are using it.

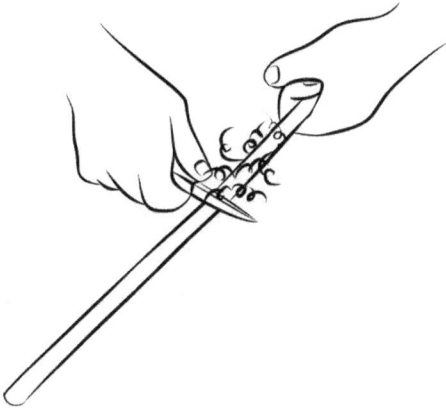

Set the broader tapered end of the spindle into the socket in the fireboard while holding it steady with your handhold on top. Now, move the bow back and forth at a steady pace until you see smoke starting to form. If the spindle hasn't jumped from the socket, then it is deep enough. If it has jumped from the socket, then go ahead and make it deeper. This is the drilling step and will ensure nothing jumps out of place when creating an ember. Th e fireboard must not move, so be sure to keep it in place by setting one of your feet on it.

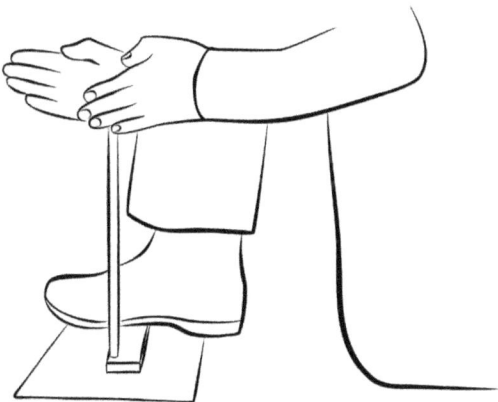

The next step is to cut a notch in the lower socket, about an eighth of the socket; this will allow the coal dust to fall on a waiting piece of bark or green leaf, igniting into an ember. This notch is to provide oxygen without the spindle leaving the socket. Ensure that all the burning materials are ready before you start. Set everything up again and move the bow back and forth to create the black dust that will birth a burning ember. As you move the bow and spindle, you will notice that smoke is rising. Lift the spindle to see if you have coal by fanning the black dust to see if it turns red. Suppose it does, then transfer it to your tinder nest. Once on the tinder, you can gently blow on it until you notice flames. Then follow the steps with the kindling until you have a fire. It may take some practice to get this right, so practice this skill before going hunting.

If you do not have a cord, you will have to make one with your shoelace or forgo the bow drill and just use the hand drill. This is where you use your hands to twist the spindle back and forth while applying pressure rather than the bow doing the work. You may need a thinner and longer spindle to achieve this by hand.

If you are injured or too exhausted, there is an easier way to make a fire if you have a cell phone with a removable battery or any other type of battery and some tinfoil. To make sure you have spare tinfoil, make sure to have some chocolate in your pack or keep some in your fire starting kit.

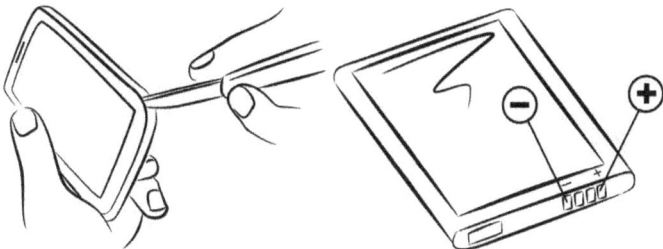

Once you have removed the battery from the phone, identify the positive and negative parts. These are marked on the battery, so it should be easy to note. Take your tinfoil and roll or fold it to create two prongs with a loop in the center. Halfway between the prongs and loop, make a bend, as this is where the tin foil will contact the battery.

(Tip: This will be fast and hot, so protect your fingers and make sure that you have your tinder ready to catch fire.)

Apply the bend in the tinfoil to the battery and set it close to your tinder. Depending on how thick you rolled your tinfoil, it may take a few seconds before you notice the smoke coming from the tinfoil. Th e charge from the battery causes the tinfoil to heat up and smoke before it eventually bursts into flame. Avoid damaging the battery if your phone is still functional.

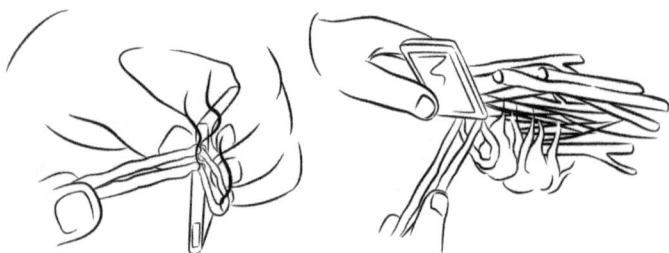

Food

The only thing missing now is the steady supply of food you require to keep your energy up as you wait for help. Your supplies will not last forever, but if it is dried, it is best to keep that for a later time when you cannot hunt or if you failed to bag something. You still have your weapon of choice, so you can still harvest food. However, ammunition does run out, and you may find that you have to rely on a backup hunting tool to still gather the food you need.

A weapon that allows you to have some distance between you and your prey is the spear. A spear can be made simply by carving a long, sturdy stick down to a point, but this is not the only way. You can also split the point to create a fork, and you can strengthen this fork by tying a wooden wedge or stone to keep the fork open. To create a three pronged spear, you can add a third sharpened stick to this and tie it in place. This can hunt several small animals you can sneak up on or barb the ends to create a fishing spear.

Hunting isn't your only means of getting a fresh food source in your general vicinity. Suppose you have taken any wildlife courses that allow you to identify different trees, plants, and mushrooms. In that case, you can also try your hand at gathering from these food sources to keep yourself going. However, if you are not familiar with a species, do not eat it at all! Some of the edible mushrooms include the morel mushrooms (which have a honeycomb-like cap), the hedgehog mushroom (also known as the sweet tooth or wood hedgehog, which have a smooth top cap but a spiky bottom), the black trumpet mushroom (which looks like a small, black trumpet), and hen-of-the-woods (also known as ram's or sheep's head, or maitake, which looks like a clump of coral) (Fratt, 2018).

There are several edible plants throughout North America, and depending on when and where you hunt, you can make use of most of them. Plants such as clover, dandelions, rosehips, wild asparagus, cattails (also known as punks), and even green seaweed or kelp are easily recognized. Most of the plants can be utilized (MacKay &

MacKay, 2020). A common rule of thumb when it comes to the safety of choosing the right plant is that you avoid anything that has a milky or discolored sap, contains spines or fine hairs, or has a bitter taste. Similarly, with mushrooms, if you cannot identify the plant with 100% accuracy, give it a complete skip. Even if you see an animal eating it, don't assume the same can be said for you eating it.

Something else that you shouldn't turn your nose up at is eating insects. As long as it isn't brightly colored, has a sting, or covered in hair, it is edible. Crickets, grasshoppers, and termites are a great source of protein and can be fried so that you can enjoy a nice crunch while you eat them. You can even eat earthworms and slugs or use them as bait for fish if you have access to a river or ocean.

(Tip: Be sure to count the legs; if it has more than six, give it a skip.)

If you are close to the ocean, look to crustaceans like crabs or other marine life such as turtles as other food sources. You are trying to survive, and you may have to let go of beliefs such as "Ew, gross! I can't eat that!" This could be your only chance to survive until help arrives. Depending on the season, you can even look for eggs or nesting birds. Clubbing a roosting or nesting bird as it sleeps is a sure way to get a meal without having to chase an animal down. Bird bones are great to make hooks with if you plan on going fishing.

Your food isn't just about fats, proteins, and carbohydrates; it is also about vitamins and minerals. Within a few days, you can start seeing the result of missing these parts in your diet. Although you can get vitamin B from eating animals and calcium from insects or crustaceans, you cannot go wrong by making some tea with fresh pine or spruce needles to give you the necessary vitamin C (Bennett, 2016).

(Tip: Keep your eyes open for anything that can help you. Trash like candy wrappers, old cans, and glass bottles can all help you survive a little longer by helping with making fire or catching water.)

CHAPTER 4

SMALL GAME FOR STARTERS

Most people aren't ready to hunt a black bear or even a moose on their first day out, so look into hunting small game animals until you have built up the confidence to tackle the larger animals. The satisfaction of hunting a squirrel is just as exciting as taking your first deer. Some small game animals in several states/provinces can be hunted year-round instead of limited to a short few days or weeks, as seen with several large game animals. As hunting is becoming more popular—and the cost of it is rising every year—the chance of getting a shot at bagging your particular quarry of choice is becoming rarer every hunting season, so hunting small game is a perfect way for you to hone your skills while you wait for those sought-after tags.

Several small animals—from squirrel size to turkey size—will be discussed in better depth in this section. These animals are likely in your backyard—please don't hunt in your backyard unless you are well away from civilization — and rarely require tags. However, check your state or provincial requirements for various licenses before picking up your hunting weapon of choice and heading out to find them. Each state/province also has its unique hunting season per particular animal, as well as how many you are allowed to hunt per day (bagging) or have on your person (holding), so be sure to brush up on this knowledge.

SQUIRREL

There are several squirrel species that you can hunt for several months of the year—usually between September and January. The bagging limit per species per day is generally between four and six. Squirrels are arboreal (tree-living) rodents with large bushy tails that come in various colors that vary from gray, black, brown, and even red. Their diet consists mainly of tree nuts, seeds, tree buds, berries, fungi (mushrooms), and even crops if they are in the area.

Squirrels are preyed upon by many different birds, reptiles, and predators. They tend only to live a few years in the wild. The areas you are likely to find squirrels—in most parts of America and Canada—are mixed forests that contain the food source they need to survive. They also like to nest, and that is one way that you can track them. Their nests are similar to that of crows but messier and contain more leaves. These animals tend to have between one and two litters a year that contain anywhere from two to four kits/pups (baby squirrels) safely cared for by the female. The gestation period (pregnancy) is about 45 days, and the kits/pups are born during the latter part of spring into summer.

Another way to track that a squirrel has been through an area is to create divots in the ground and snow looking for their cache of stored food. Although squirrels are known for hiding their food, they do not always remember where it was hidden and are likely to use another squirrel's cache as much as their own.

Squirrels can be hunted in three ways: spot-and-stalk, stop-and-go hunting, and ambush hunting. The best time to hunt them is in the morning—not too early as they do not like the cold—and evenings. As a beginner, an excellent way to start hunting them is to simply sit at the base of a tree and wait, listening for their movements. They are not known to be quiet as they run through the trees. Squirrel is quite edible and has dark meat that tastes similar to chicken but is somewhat tougher yet full of flavor. You can drop this prey with either a .22 rifle—aim for the head—or a shotgun with #6 pellets. If you are confident, you can try a slingshot if the squirrel is on the ground. Learning to hunt squirrels will sharpen your skills in stalking and patience while you get to enjoy the beautiful view.

RABBIT

Rabbit season includes rabbits and hares. The two animals are vastly different, but the easiest way to remember the difference is that a hare is born above ground, fully furred, and ready to run. Meanwhile, a rabbit is born underground in a warren, naked, blind, and requires constant care from its mother.

Depending on which state or province you find yourself in, hares and rabbits may be hunted year-round, while other species of rabbits, you can only hunt during the fall and winter. Unlike pet rabbits, the wild varieties tend to be dull browns and grays, while the cottontails have a white underbelly and under tail with rust-colored fur around the neck. Generally, hunting licenses for these animals are affordable. It is very much worth it, as this meat is worth the hunt. Cottontail especially is excellent, as it can be treated the same way as chicken yet manages to have its unique flavor.

Their diet consists of most things vegetative, but they will resort to eating bark during the winter. They have several predators that hunt them, including animals such as mink, bobcats, and birds of prey that fly by night and day. If a predator can chase the rabbit, it gets to eat it. The standard life span is less than four years, but a female can have up to five litters a year with as many as nine kittens. Both rabbits and hares prefer thick grass or brush so that they can hide.

However, those from the western parts of the U.S.A. find shelter more often in rocky outcrops.

Signs of passing are generally the running trails and dropping these animals leave behind, but you can also note where the bark has been chewed off of trees. If checking the brush, look for plant stems that have been eaten, as they tend to have a very sharp angle due to the teeth of these animals.

Primarily, these creatures are nocturnal due to the number of predators that eat them, and they will avoid open areas where possible. The best time to hunt rabbits is in the morning and evenings where they will be lounging around the entrance of their warrens. There are several ways to hunt rabbits. If the state/province allows it, you can use snares over the entrance of the warren or in their trail runs. Generally, the spot-and-stalk method is best, and you will only get a single chance to shoot, as they are jumpy animals and will run for their warrens if spooked. Rifles and shotguns can be used.

GROUSE

A grouse is a type of pheasant that comes in various colors, including brown, gray (found in colder places), red (found in warmer areas), and even white. Hunting season on these birds is between September and December, and the bag limit may depend on which grouse you want to hunt. A grouse can easily be identified separately from a partridge. They tend to have small feathers in their nostrils and their legs covered up with feathers until their toes.

Many species are found in both forests and mountains and are a prize for any hunter's plate. While Spruce and Greater-Sage Grouse tend to taste like the plants they eat — and their namesake—the Ruffed Grouse has sweet white meat similar to lean chicken, while the Sharp-tailed Grouse and Rock Ptarmigan tend to have dark meat that is gamey and similar to duck. With that being said, pick your flavor and go hunting for it.

The diet of these birds varies from catkins, buds, twigs, soft fruits, ferns, acorns, and even insects. Reptiles, birds, and mammals feed on the adult grouse as easily as they do the juveniles and eggs. A female grouse can lay anywhere from eight to 14 buff-colored eggs, which can take up to two days to lay a clutch. It takes up to 26 days to incubate all the eggs. The hatchlings can immediately start foraging for food and can fly within five days. Nests are generally made up of depressed leaves close to cover so the female can watch for predators.

These birds may have to be flushed from hiding so you can make use of dogs to aid in this, or you can walk around trying to find them yourself. A smaller gauge shotgun is perfect for hunting these tiny birds. You will know you are in grouse territory because the males drum their wings to attract females. You will need to keep an eye out to find them.

PARTRIDGE

Although a little smaller than most grouse, the partridge family boasts far more colors, especially the males. The barring recognizes these birds on their legs and the gorgeous(black mask) over their eyes. Their legs are featherless and, depending on the species, can either be bright red or orange. These birds like the open areas such as farmlands and grassy fields, so spotting them is quite possible while walking.

When hunting with dogs, these birds tend to flush downhill then run uphill, so look out for that if you are hunting with a dog. You will have to do quite a bit of walking to get the perfect shot. The diet of these birds consists of grains and seeds with a side of insects if available. The female will lay between 12 and 18 olive-colored eggs, which will hatch during June up until late July. Upon hatching, the chicks will start to forage on their own. Similar to the grouse, these birds are also accosted by many birds, mammals, and reptilian predators that will eat them during their life cycle.

To track these animals, look along a farm's field edge or even roadsides for them. They like to hide in sparse cover or short grass along these borders. They tend to feed out in the open during the early morning and late afternoon while spending the rest of the day wandering around. These birds are more easily hunted with a smaller gauge shotgun.

Hunting season on these birds is between September and January. Your bag limit can be anything from four to eight a day. Their meat is somewhat darker than most bird species—though the breast meat is still white—but is rather tasty with a mild flavor.

QUAIL

This is probably the smallest of the bird species that you will hunt for food. In the eastern parts of the U.S.A., these birds tend to live in grasslands and pine forests while they live in more mountainous or even desert locations in the West. Regardless of where they live, they are ground-dwelling birds. They do not have very good endurance for flying yet are excellent runners. These birds will fly up in groups if startled, so many hunters like to use dogs when seeking out this bird.

Most of the quail species tend to be dull grayish. Some can even have red, black, or white feathers mixed in. They also tend to have plumage that looks similar to scales on their chest. A female will lay between 12 and 16 eggs between April and June and take about 23 days to hatch. The food of choice for these birds is seeds, berries, any available fruit in the area, and insects. They can live up to three years in the wild.

Hunting season starts in October and ends in February—the same months vary from place to place—and the bag limit is usually up to eight. They are tasty birds with their own unique flavored white meat. The use of a .410 bore is perfect for this bird. However, note that there are protected quail as they are being endangered due to habitat loss. Ensure where and what you are hunting to give those endangered a fighting chance to get their numbers up.

DUCKS

Several duck species can be hunted all over Canada, America, and even Mexico. One of the most popular is the mallard. These birds are so sought after that they are very predictable—as some are migratory—and they have high-quality meat that many people enjoy. The coloration of ducks can vary from browns, whites, blacks, and even bright colors such as blues and greens. Generally, the males are brighter in color than their female companions. This is a good thing as most states/provinces regulate the hunting of females more than males.

Hunting season for ducks extends from September to February, and bag limits vary from location to location. As these are aquatic birds (waterfowl), you will find them at any body of water which includes but is not limited to ponds, lakes, ditches with water, and reservoirs. Ducks that do migrate do it to remain close to liquid water. Their diet consists of aquatic plants and many crops. Insects are usually only eaten during the mating season to build up protein reserves for laying eggs.

As ducks spend time on both land and water, their predators include reptiles, mammals, birds, and large fish, taking the juveniles with ease. Despite having many predators, most ducks can live up to a decade or more in the wild. Females typically lay clutches of between one and 13 eggs—at a rate of roughly one egg a day—between February and May. These eggs incubate for between 23 and 33 days.

Ducks can easily be tracked, as you can see their tracks in the mud surrounding the water and several feathers in the general vicinity. When you hunt for a duck can be heavily dependent on what role the weather plays, but generally, morning and late afternoon are good times to start your hunt. There are many ways to hunt ducks, from stalking to using duck calls and decoys. A smaller gauge shotgun is once again best to use when hunting duck, but any weapon you have a good aim with is good enough.

TURKEY

This is the largest of the birds you will hunt in America. Several species of these birds vary in dark colors with a few feathers that are bronze, green, or even copper. The necks are featherless, while the males have spurred legs, either blue or redheads, and they have a tuft of feathers on the chest called a beard. The females can also have this beard but to a lesser effect and have dull feathers. Both sexes have white-tipped rump and tail feathers.

Turkeys have excellent eyesight, so you will have to wear camouflage—with orange if the state/province requires it—and make use of stalking tactics as well as using the necessary calls to attract the birds. The habitat of these birds can vary from desert to savanna, with the birds preferring grasslands to feed and mate and forests to roost and avoid predators. Sure signs of turkey in the area include dusting bowls and scratch marks of feeding.

A turkey's diet varies from nuts, fruits, seeds, grasses, crops, insects, snails, and small rodents. They can live up to five years and are preyed upon by various nest raiders and predators such as mountain lions for the adults and owls for the younger birds. The female lays up to 12 eggs at a rate of an egg a day. Incubation only starts after the last egg is laid so that the whole clutch can be born within 28 days. Turkey season is split into a fall season—where both sexes are hunted—and a spring season, where only the male is hunted. Usually, turkey hunting is from sunrise to sunset, and you will need tags to hunt them.

The turkey can be quartered the same as a chicken and contains white breast meat, while the legs, wings, and thighs are of darker, tougher meat. You can also make use of the giblets such as the gizzard, heart, and liver if you are so inclined. There are strict laws on hunting turkey, so check your regulations before picking up a favored weapon.

BULLFROG

Bullfrogs are one of the largest frogs in the world, up to six inches in length. You will need to keep an eye on the regulations of the state/province you are in. In some, this animal is an invasive species, and you can hunt them freely, while others have a bag limit. The hunting season for bullfrogs is unique and widely different in each state/province.

The bullfrogs vary in color from brown, greenish-gray, light olive, or yellowish-green with a large external eardrum. They also have large webbed hind feet. They are omnivorous as well as cannibalistic and will not hesitate to eat other bullfrogs when hungry. They live in areas that have permanent water sources for their breeding, living, and feeding. Females lay up to 10,000 eggs that will hatch within two to five days. The tadpole usually overwinters in the mud and will transform into adult frogs when the weather starts to warm, but this can also take up to two years to complete. Even the adults overwinter in the mud. They have many predators that cover most of the animal kingdom.

These frogs are active day and night, although most people prefer to hunt them by night. They are easily traceable through their loud sounds, so a sit-and-wait tactic is best to use. They can be hunted with spears, bows, and even a gig (a type of fish spear). The best part of the frog to eat is the legs—fried, grilled, or boiled—with a taste and texture similar to chicken.

SNAPPING TURTLE

This is likely the most dangerous of the small game you will get to hunt. This large reptile (as large as 68 pounds), with its protective shell, saw-toothed scales, and long tail (longer in males than females), has a large head on a long neck with a beak that can remove fingers if you are not careful. As this animal likes to hide in weed-choked permanent wetlands in the mud, their coloration tends to vary from black to light brown. They are an opportunistic feeder that will eat anything from carrion to fresh plant matter.

They will hibernate during winter under logs or in the mud, either singularly or as a community. The female will lay between 20 and 40 eggs per clutch in gravel pits or soil banks, then she will leave. These turtles are very vulnerable on land, as they cannot pull their head or limbs into their shells. Hunting season is generally between July and March, avoiding the mating and egg-laying season. These animals can be hunted in several ways, such as traps (if allowed in the state/province), hooks, or even nets. You will need to distract the head—get a sturdy stick— to grab the tail if you want to avoid receiving a painful bite. The animal can be quartered and cooked exactly like chicken, though its meat is a little darker in color.

LARGER PREY

As your skills grow, you may want to move onto larger prey and maybe even hunt other predators. You can hunt many species that will be discussed at length in another book, but here is a taste of what is available to you.

Deer

The season for hunting deer (between July and February) is limited by the weapon you choose to use (muzzleloader, crossbows, bows, and general guns), zones within the location, and various states or provinces. These animals are used for meat, pelts, and even trophies.

Moose

This is one of the biggest animals you will get to hunt, as it towers over 7.5 feet and weighs in at 1,800 pounds. Usually, the hunting season is from September to October. Still, some states/provinces will stop the season if there isn't a stable population of this animal. Even if there is a stable population, the tags are awarded through a lottery system.

Bear

This hunting season is from mid-October to early January. How you hunt—hounds, spot-and-stalk, or bait—the bear varies significantly from place to place. Tags are required, and you can either use a gun or a bow. Bear is edible—as it is an omnivore—but it is dependent on the location and the time of the year.

Wolf

In 2019, you could only hunt wolves as trophies in Alaska, Montana, Idaho, and Wyoming—each having its duration for the hunting season—and in other states/provinces, they were heavily protected. However, as of January 4th, 2021, the gray wolf was delisted as a protected species. The hunting season for these animals will start as of November 2021. Until such time, the only reason you are allowed to kill a wolf is if it is on your property and it is attacking you, your pets, or livestock.

CHAPTER 5

IDENTIFYING SIGNS AND TRACKS

U nless you physically see the animal you want to hunt before you, you will need to track them to find where they are. Each animal has a unique track and signs that it leaves behind as it moves through its territory. A true hunter will use what is left behind to stalk and get the quarry they are after. Similar animals leave similar signs, so be sure to use your eyes and ears to note the animal to ensure that you are hunting the correct one.

Tracking isn't just about what you see before you. You need to be sure of what is around you at all times. This is not only for your safety but also to ensure that you remain within your hunting license's specifications. You cannot hunt an animal that crosses outside of the area allowed to hunt in. You also cannot cross over into posted private property. So yes, keep an eye on the signs, and ensure that you know what is happening in your general vicinity.

AGE OF TRACKS

It is pointless to follow tracks that are days old, so you need to be sure of the age of the track before setting off in a direction. Tracks are subjected to many factors which can cause them to look newer or older. If tracks are covered by leaves or dust, think about when it was windy. If the tracks are in mud or snow, then step next to it and compare your tracks with the animal's tracks to see how different they look from each other. Sharp edges to the track mean that it is fresh. However, when tracking in snow, this can be a bit misleading due to the possibility of the top layer melting and freezing, giving it the appearance of being fresh. Compare tracks that are found in direct sunlight with those made in the shade. Those in the shade tend to be more accurate, as they would have been less exposed to being melted and refreezing.

WHEN TO TRACK

The best time to track an animal depends on where you want to shoot it. Suppose you are tracking an animal in the morning. In that case, you are likely to find it laying down to rest—depending on the species—while tracking later in the afternoon, and you could find the animal feeding. Knowing what to expect from the animal will allow you to make decisions, such as going toward a bedded area where the animal may be resting or getting ahead of the tracks to wait for the animal to reach its feeding grounds. The longer you practice your stalking techniques, the better you will become at it.

SQUIRREL

As these are tree-dwelling creatures, you can count yourself very lucky if you manage to find their tracks. The prints left behind look similar to those of rats with a longer hind foot than the forefoot. Th e size of the footprints is dependent on the species of squirrel you are hunting. The hind foot has five toes each, while the forefoot has four.

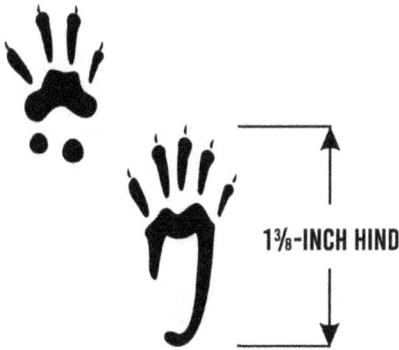

1⅜-INCH HIND

SQUIRREL

Squirrels are known as gallopers or hoppers, which means when they walk, their hind feet will move in front of their forefeet. They will also keep their feet together as they move, and you may not necessarily see the heel of their hind feet, so keep an eye on the number of toes you can count. The hind footprints will also point slightly outward. Other signs of squirrels include chewed nut husks and holes dug where they are looking for or burying their nut caches. Their droppings are easily recognizable—as though they may seem similar to rat droppings—and they are larger and barrel-shaped. They do not end in a taper like their rodent cousins. Th ese droppings can be found at the foot of trees in little piles or singularly.

RABBIT

Rabbits, such as cottontails, have hairy feet, so it is a little more difficult to count the number of toes. However, they also have an elongated back foot—measuring 3–4 inches— and a smaller, round forefoot measuring about an inch. A jackrabbit's paws are a little bigger and have less fur on the underside of their feet, so with their tracks, you can see four toes in the front and four toes in the back.

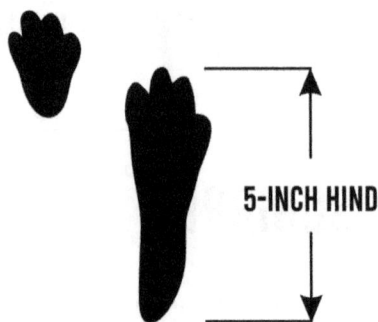

5-INCH HIND

JACKRABBIT

Similar to squirrels, rabbits are also gallopers or hoppers. However, their feet tend to be more staggered than squirrels, and they do not always align with each other. The tracks of cottontails, snowshoe hares, and jackrabbits are identical in shape though sizes vary between the species. Rabbit scat can be found wherever the animal is resting or eating and are generally round, semi-dry droppings that form a small pile. Softer, darker droppings that are clumped together may be noted from time to time. Other ways to track these animals while on a hunt is with lights (spotlighting) where you note the eyeshine. However, this way of hunting may be illegal in many states/provinces, so check your regulations before attempting it. Keep an eye out for feeding damage by rabbits, such as ring barking (where a ring around the base of trees is missing bark) and plants being chewed off at a sharp angle.

UPLAND BIRDS

Upland wild game birds—these being the grouse, partridge, and quail—all have similar tracks and behaviors. However, their size, shape, and coloration may be different.

GROUSE   1¾ INCHES   QUAIL   1¾ INCHES

Birds that tend to spend most of their life on the ground have three toes pointing forward in a W-like shape, while they may have one small toe pointing backward, though this may be completely missing in some upland birds. When escaping predators, these birds prefer to fly for short distances and run for most. Their track patterns tend to be alternative—one track followed by another ahead of it—in a straight line as they move. Another sign that you may notice is the dusting bowls. To rid themselves of parasites on their skin or feathers, these birds will burrow with their underbellies into the soft sand to smother or remove them. The size of these dust bowls is dependent on the species creating them. Any lost feathers you find while hunting down the birds will also help you determine what species is in the area. Unless you are using dogs that will help point out or flush these birds from their hiding spot, you will need to do a lot of walking and keeping your eyes open to find them.

DUCKS

Like most birds that do not roost in trees, ducks also have three forward-facing toes. They have no toes facing backward but rather have webbing between each of the toes. You can often find these tracks along muddy banks, but they can be a little challenging to follow, as the ducks do like to wander around quite a bit and create a maze of tracks that are difficult to read. When walking in a straight line, ducks have an alternative pattern to their tracks. Feathers in the area may also give you a clue about where the animals are bedding down for the night.

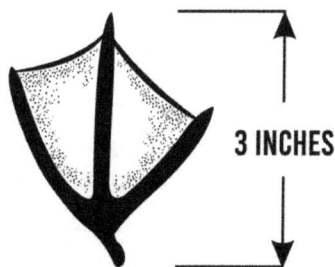

3 INCHES

MALLARD DUCK

When hunting ducks, you want the animal to come to you, as shooting it over the water without a dog to retrieve it is nothing more than a wasted kill. It will sink if you do not retrieve it quickly. This is why many hunters prefer to lie in wait for ducks with buffs or among decoys while they sit in camouflage clothing with calls. It is illegal to bait most animals in America, so don't even think of it as a way to attract ducks. Another way to track ducks is to become familiar with their migration patterns and then look into the sky to locate them.

(Tip: By following the general direction that ducks fly in, you will be able to find their natural feeding areas and can thus stalk them from a vehicle for some distance before continuing on foot.)

TURKEY

The turkey is also an upland bird, but its tracks are significantly bigger than the grouse, partridge, and quail. Its tracks—three toes point forward, with the middle toe being considerably larger than the others—can be as large as four inches. The males have larger feet than the females. As these birds do roost at night, they have a longer fourth toe—which isn't always seen in the tracks—pointing backward to help grip the tree branch while they sleep. When leaping down from the trees, the tracks will show a side-by-side formation of the feet—similarly to birds that hop when moving from one place to another—but when it starts to move away, the tracks start to alternate.

4 INCHES

WILD TURKEY

Other signs you can look for are the salad bowl-sized dust bowls they create and the wing drag marks the gobblers (males) create when facing off against a rival, as well as the scratchings as they look for food.

As with all birds that you track, the open ends of the toes point in the direction that the bird is going, so it is important to count the toes to ensure that you are going the right way. Turkey droppings can also identify which of the genders left it behind. This is very important to a hunter as the gender allowed to be hunted for a specific season can then be identified and then tracked. The males tend to leave long droppings—about two inches in length—that form a

J-like shape. Th is is because they are always on the move and don't even stop to do their business. The hens, however, don't move as much and tend to leave piles that are curled more than the males' droppings.

BULLFROG

No surprise, but bullfrogs are also hoppers, and when they are moving around, their hind feet will land either next to their forefeet or slightly in front of them. The hind feet end in five bulbous toes, and the forelegs end in four, with both feet being webbed for swimming. The forefeet are slightly turned inward while the hind feet are turned outward. Depending on how soft the mud is, you may be lucky enough to see the webbing of the feet, but this is not always the case, and you are more likely only to see the toes. Sometimes you can even see the belly imprint as the creature hops from place to place.

(Tip: As they like to be buried in the mud or floating in the water when not looking for food, you may have to disturb their area a little to help locate them if your eyes are not that sharp.)

2 INCHES

BULLFROG

SNAPPING TURTLE

Snapping turtles have massive feet and claws, so their tracks are obvious to see, and the size of the print will depend on the animal's age. With five claws in the back and four in the front, it isn't just their beak that can hurt you if you do not handle these creatures with the respect they deserve. As the turtle moves on land, you will mostly see its claws and not the webbing as well as the drag marks from its underbelly and its tail. Scat from this animal is usually found in soft, loose, and pie-like forms on land, and if it is in the water, it simply washes away and is rarely seen. These turtles like to hide during the day when tired and come out at night. When hiding, they burrow into the mud along the edges of their watery home, creating a bowl-like shape that rises from the mud. A hunter with a sturdy stick can push it through the mound, and if it makes contact with a shell, there is a distinct knocking sound.

1 INCH

TURTLE

OTHER POSSIBLE SIGNS

As you are hunting small game, don't miss the opportunity to scout for the larger game for the next season. By noting these tracks, you can make plans to revisit the area once you have the confidence built up to hunt the larger animals.

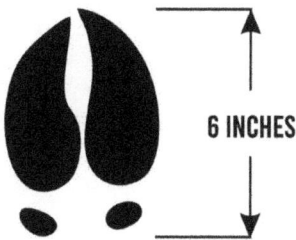

6 INCHES

3 INCHES

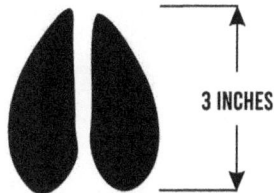

MOOSE   WHITE-TAILED DEER

The moose can be particularly dangerous, so try to avoid them unless you are actively hunting them. They can and do kill humans every year, so be cautious. Although the white-tailed deer and moose prints are similar, you cannot overlook the sheer size difference.

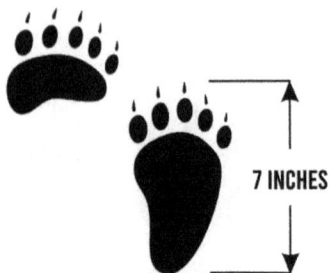

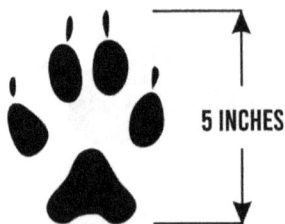

BLACK BEAR **GRAY WOLF**

Not just that, but if there are predators in the area that you are not prepared to come across and want to avoid, you can do so by going in the opposite of the tracks. Although most predators will not attack a human directly if there are youngsters in the area, you are exposing yourself to a possible attack. Let this be the warning the animal may not give you.

CHAPTER 6

BETTER SCOUT MORE THAN YOU HUNT

Learning how to scout is the best tool in a hunter's bag of tricks. Being able to understand the nature of animals makes hunting them far easier and more enjoyable. Instead of walking for hours and getting nothing, you can keep your eyes peeled for little hints about what has been moving through the area. Whether you are tracking squirrels or rabbits, you might notice signs of other animals that you may get more enjoyment from hunting and just so happen to have the correct tags.

It also prevents you from becoming single-minded in your endeavor to only concentrate on one thing. You are not the only person out there that is tracking, and you are not the only predator. By keeping a wary eye out, you can keep yourself in the hunter's seat and not become prey yourself to animals like mountain lions, bears, and even wolves. By knowing your prey and their habits, you will know what they do to survive and therefore have an opportunity to see into their lives and build a mental picture of their potential movements and needs. Scouting allows you to stalk and find prey, but it is not easy and requires a lot of practice to hone this particular skill.

SCOUTING FROM A DISTANCE

Scouting does not start when you hit the trail with all your gear. If this is how you plan on scouting, there will be a lot of walking in your future. Whether you are hunting deer or rabbits, you need to know where they are before stumbling into the wilderness. Not just that, but you also need to know and become familiar with the terrain that you will be moving through before you start to do that. Unless you are a veteran hunter that has decades of notes and maps of their best hunting spots, you will need to start your scouting adventure behind the screen of a computer.

Suppose you are going to make use of public hunting grounds. In that case, you will need to identify the best possible place where your prey may be roaming. You can do that through viewing aerial photos, Google Earth, or simply taking the time to join a hunter's forum to get the necessary information from those that have years of experience under their belts. Many hunters will be willing to share a rough estimate of where some of the better hunting grounds are, but don't expect them to tell you where their best hunting spots are, as that is usually a closely guarded secret. You can even make use of resources like YouTube to see the kind of terrain you are likely to find where your particular prey may be hiding. However, keep in mind that those 20-minute videos are usually made after days of scouting, stalking, and finding the perfect opportunity to take the prey. They make a long process look easy, and it doesn't always give the whole scope of the hunt.

Scouting digitally gives a person from out of state/province an opportunity to look at what the general hunting area will look like. You may need to factor in seasonal changes depending on where you are hunting and when you started your digital scouting. Although you could spot terrain perfect for hunting, remember that you are not the only one with this information. Thousands are looking at the same data as you. You will need to plan accordingly if several people want to hunt the same area, so be sure to scout several locations. Having several sites to visit will help you avoid areas that other hunters saturate.

You can also have a partner that can look at the photos and give their own opinion on what they see, and the two of you can work together to choose the best place to hunt. You can even pull in a veteran hunter to help you with some tips and tricks, but be sure to treat them to a hot coffee as thanks for parting with the knowledge. However, no matter how well you scout online or from photos, it is not good to rely solely on this information, as you will have no idea what is happening on the ground. Your next step is to put boots on the ground and scout in person off-season as well as while you hunt.

SCOUTING OFF-SEASON

This is not always possible for a hunter that has to travel to a different state/province, but it is a valued experience that you should not turn your nose up at. Having boots on the ground allows you to see what the terrain is like, which may not have been clear from the aerial photos. Knowing the animal habits you are planning on hunting will give you the edge to your hunting, as you will know what to look for as you walk the vicinity. As you are hiking and looking around, be sure to mark areas of interest on your map so that you can return to them when the season is in full swing.

Check all the potential areas you have identified as points of interest in your online searches to see what the physical location looks like. In reality, these areas may no longer be as good as they appeared online, but now you can scout better areas while you are there. This is how you gain experience. Everything is a learning opportunity. There is no such thing as the perfect hunting ground. Animals keep moving to find better feeding, mating, and resting areas, and you will need to move after them to learn of these places so that you can always find them. Hunting is about more scouting than actually pulling a trigger or laying traps. If you do not know the land and your particular prey's habits, you will never get an opportunity to have one in your sight while you aim.

SCOUTING WHILE HUNTING

If you plan on scouting during your hunting trip, be prepared to lose many hours or even days finding the perfect spot. Try to hunt in the mornings and evenings while scouting around midday, as this is when most animals are not active. Don't assume that you will always get to bag your prey on your first day—though this is a possibility—as you may need to stalk certain prey if you are not sitting and waiting for it to come to you. However, it is not only animal signs you need to note when scouting but also human signs. If there are many cars parked in the vicinity, you know there are other hunters on the trail, and you will need to be careful.

Another critical thing to remember is that tracks belong to no one. Just because you noticed them doesn't mean the animal at the end of them belongs to you. Use some common courtesy, and don't stalk an animal that is already—and obviously—being stalked by another hunter. Suppose you are using ambush tactics for animals, and there are other hunters in the area. In that case, it is a good idea to move at least 100 yards from them so as not to impact their hunting experience. Remember, animals don't like too much activity—especially from humans—so seek to avoid other people by hunting deeper into the wilderness.

This can be a double-edged sword, though. Heading deeper into the wilderness may yield higher success, but if you are hunting larger prey—say turkeys—you may find carrying your prize back a tedious task that takes a lot out of you. This is especially true for people who hunt larger animals such as deer, elk, and bears. As you are wandering around, always be aware of boundaries to the properties in the vicinity. The best way to prevent accidental trespassing is to contact all the private landowners and make them aware of your presence and get the necessary permission to be on their property. If this is not possible, always check and re-check your map to ensure you are where you are supposed to be.

Then, after all that hard work, you have a successful hunt. Congratulations, but keep the celebrations down as much as possible. You may have been lucky, but some-one else may still be trying, and you do not want to ruin their opportunity. This is just common courtesy, after all. Another courtesy is that you do not dress (butcher) your kill on the path where others may see it. Move away from where others may be. This brings us to the final point of scouting. Pick up after yourself! No true hunter leaves trash in their wake, only their footprints.

(Tip: These are general scouting tips that can be used on a variety of animals, but for them to work specifically on the animal you want to hunt, you will also need to incorporate what you know about them to find, stalk, and ambush them.)

SQUIRRELS

Squirrels love white oak acorns but will not turn up their nose at any other nut source. If you want to find squirrels, then find their food source. Once you have noted their food source, look to see if there are signs of squirrels such as tracks or husks of nuts that have already been eaten. If there is a stable food source, they will not go far, and you can simply sit and wait for them to return in case you have spooked them with your entrance into their territory. Nuts are not the only food that they use, so look for patches of edible mushrooms and berries they may eat.

Squirrels spook easily, so hunt them slowly. Take a few steps, then listen. Squirrels make a lot of noise, such as gnawing, dropping nuts, or scampering along branches. Even if you do not hear any close to you, you will be able to listen to some farther away and can therefore stalk them. Even when spooked, squirrels will return to where there is food. You just need to be patient.

Take a seat and wait. If you have a pair of binoculars, now is the time to take them out and scout the area to see where possible squirrels are hiding in trees watching you. If you are quiet and limit your movement, these animals will return to the area within about 40 minutes or so. Line up your shot when you have selected your target, and then take it.

If you want to continue hunting squirrels after taking a shot—either successful or not—you can move to another location a few hundred yards away and try your luck again. Squirrels are active around sunrise and sunset and will actively avoid being out and about during bad weather.

RABBITS

Sadly, with the way humans are encroaching on wild animals' territories, the vast grasslands for hunting rabbits are few and far between. You will have to use a technique called leapfrogging to move from place to place when looking for rabbits or hares. Scouting rabbits is relatively easy using binoculars from a car when driving along roads close to fields and farms. The best time to do this is during dawn and dusk. If you notice rabbits on private property—especially on farms—speak to the farmer about what you have seen. Most farmers will only be too happy to have a rabbit problem disappear without them having to do anything about it. Offering to share the spoils of your hunt wouldn't be a bad gesture on your part as a thank you.

When you have permission to go onto the land, scout it as well. Look for areas that contain brush, fallen treetops, or even brush piles for where rabbits like to hide. Many things eat rabbits, so they are likely to hide and stay hidden until disturbed. You will need to drive them into more open areas to get better opportunities to take them accurately. These animals' coats offer excellent camouflage, so they may be difficult to spot. Don't look for a body; look for the eyes. Glossy spheres are not seen in nature, so if you see them, you know you have a rabbit. If you spot a rabbit this way, you can make use of the spot-and-stalk method, getting just close enough to take an accurate shot.

Rabbits can be tricky to flush on your own. Still, if you use the stop-and-go method, it is a great way to stress the animal into fleeing from you if you have not seen a rabbit take a few heavy steps and then wait. Rabbits can't handle that pressure; if they think they have been spotted, they will bolt. When they do this, you can take a shot. However, some rabbits will try to hold on until your back is to them. Then, they will scamper off to safety, or when they flee successfully, they will try to circle back to avoid you. Always glance over your shoulder now and again to see if any rabbits have done this. Similar to squirrels, if you have flushed all the rabbits and can't spot them anymore, then stop, sit down, and wait for them to return to the safe area.

UPLAND BIRDS

Although the tracks of most upland birds look the same, their natural habitats are all a little different, and this will aid you in scouting them. As these birds are shot on the wing, it is a good idea to practice skeet shooting. This practice will allow you to focus on hitting a moving target that travels through the air. The use of well-trained pointers and receivers is generally permitted when hunting these animals but not required. With a bit of leg work on your part, you can do this alone or with a human partner.

Grouse

These birds like to make use of young forests as homes. These types of forests have different plants that can offer them the cover required to avoid predators. You are more likely to find grouse coverts—where the birds like to congregate— at the edges of different land transitions. This could be an old forest leading into a new one or a path with gravel splits a forest. Grouse like to eat grit from these paths, so make a note if you see one.

To find a grouse, you will need to look for the food they like to eat. As the season changes, so do their food source, so look for different plants, berries, and seeds that are in season. Grouse can camouflage well, and without a dog to point them out, it will take some walking for you to be able to find them. To flush out a grouse from hiding, try the stop-and-go method of hunting. Wait about 30 seconds to a minute before starting to move again. Nervous grouse will leap into the air as they attempt to flee—though some will run—and this will be your opportunity to take a shot. Very rarely will you get a chance to aim and shoot with pinpoint accuracy. If a shot was unsuccessful, move to a new area.

Partridge

Partridge, like the chukar, like to have rocky outcrops to hide in and duck away from most predators. These structures offer crevices where they can find food as well as various places to hide. They will also hide their nests under different bushes, such as sage or greasewood, but any bushy vegetation will do. These birds like to be active in the early morning before moving into shaded areas to wait out the heat of the day. Their roosting spots are generally in steep areas that prevent predators from just sneaking up on them while they sleep.

These birds are easily stalked if you have a set of binoculars that can point out roosting or feeding areas from a distance. They are also quite chatty birds and will communicate with other birds in their convoy, so keep your ears sharp. You can even make use of a call to get birds close to you to respond. Then, it is a simple stop-and-go until the bird flushes out.

As the partridge is prone to flying down a hill and running up, the best way to hunt it is to approach it from higher ground and wait for it to fly up. As you will be shooting downhill, this may affect your aim, so get some practice in this way of shooting. If you have a dog with you, have it chase the birds toward you. Don't be too concerned if your shot misses, as there are other convoys in the vicinity. Move further up and circle around, continuing the stop-and-go method until you find your next target.

Quail

These little birds like different habitats depending on both the weather and what time of the day it is. You are likely to see several quail after it rains as they like to eat the bugs that come out. Due to this, the best time to hunt them is after some rain and the wind has calmed down considerably. If it is in the morning or late afternoon, you will likely find them in open fields looking for food to eat. If this is the case, you can stalk them until you are ready to take the shot. During midday, the birds prefer to hide in wooded areas—where there are briar patches—as predators or hunters can't spot them. At night, they are asleep in the long grass.

When looking over fields that may hold quail, look at the length and thickness of the grass. If it is too short or too thick, they do not like to enter it, as they will either be spotted or cannot move through it. As with the other upland birds, the stop-and-go method is the best to spook the bird into flight so that you can take a snapshot at it. Always make use of some binoculars if you want to scout a field without entering it, as you do not want the birds to flee into wooded areas where it is difficult to flush them out on your own.

DUCKS

There are several ways to stalk ducks, depending on your particular style of hunting. If you prefer your prey to come to you, then make use of a blind that you can hide in a while using duck calls and decoys in the body of water you are hunting on. Ducks are more likely to use bodies of water that already contain ducks, as they are pretty social. If you want to be out on the water yourself, you can row a boat into the middle of a large body of water and then sit with the decoys and use the calls. This is called float hunting. However, when shooting a duck over the water, there is a chance that the body becomes difficult to retrieve, especially if you do not have a retriever dog. Unfortunately, the blind setup and decoys can make for a costly hunt, so because of this, most hunters prefer the stop-and-stalk method—also known as jump shoot—which is significantly cheaper.

When you are moving more, you can identify multiple possible places where ducks like to feed, wander, or roost during the night. Ducks will use any body of water which includes places like ditches next to the road or dugout areas on farms, so always keep an eye out when traveling for potential areas that may contain duck-friendly water locations. When you spot a possible feeding area for ducks, use a pair of binoculars to see if any ducks hang around. When you spot them, you can steadily make your way toward them but will need to start stalking within 100 yards of the birds. If you have cover closer to your prey, all the better, but if not, take it slow and drop to your belly. Once you are within a range, you are comfortable taking a shot. Then, you can stand up to reveal yourself. This should cause the ducks to flush, but if they don't, then just make some kind of noise to alert them. As they flush, aim for a duck along the edges of the group, and aim for the body to avoid shooting over or under the animal. If you missed your shot, the animals would likely return after a while, as they will need to continue to feed. This is usually easier if there is some cover for you to meld back.

When the animals are feeding, they are not always alert, so it is easier to sneak up on them. When they are wandering, closer toward the afternoon, they will be more on high alert, as they will be socializing with other ducks. If you miss a shot at this time, they are likely not to return. Shooting at ducks that are getting ready to roost poses the problem of accidentally shooting outside of the state or province's regulations. Many hunters like to set alarms for themselves that will stop them from exceeding this time limit.

Retrieval of your successful hunt can be tricky with a duck, as you would prefer to shoot the animal over the land, but this is not always the case. You cannot leave a potentially wounded animal to drown or wander deeper into the brush, so make sure to follow up as soon as you can.

TURKEY

Hunting turkey can be done in two ways. Hide in a blind with decoys and turkey callers or walking out on foot in turkey country. Both of these have their pros and cons. Turkeys have excellent eyesight, and with one false step, they will be gone in a blink of an eye. The first step to a successful turkey hunt is that you wear the appropriate camouflage for the season. The next is to decide which type of call you will use. The two most popular hands-free varieties are the mouth (diaphragm) call and the friction call. The mouth call can be purchased and held inside the mouth and will remain silent until you create the correct shape of your tongue to make the sounds required. This is something that will need to be practiced to produce the proper sounds necessary. The friction call can be made with a magnet—a product called the magnetic push/pull box call—that can be placed on the side of the shotgun and then moved when a call is required. These calls are needed, as you will need to get the turkey to come to you. Do not make calls too often, as this can cause turkeys to become wary of you.

When using a blind, make sure to set it up in an area not under a roosting tree. Turkeys move away from their roosting spots, so they may not want to hang around after waking up. Make sure you have the appropriate, natural cover around you. You want to see the turkey coming toward you, but you don't want the turkey to know where you are. Set your decoy turkeys within the range of your gun and slightly off-center of where you are. You want the wild turkey to focus on them and not your possible movement.

If you are stalking in an open country, do so slowly, and don't let a turkey spot you before you spot it. Make use of cover when you notice it, and use your calls to bring it closer. Suppose you have managed to spook the turkey you are hunting. In that case, you may have to give the area about 30 minutes of silence and no movement before starting again. If no turkey answers your call, you will have to go through to a new location and begin again. Stick to infrequent calls until you hear an answer.

Depending on the season you are hunting in, you may have to use different calls to attract the different genders. When making the gobble sound, you are likely to attract large males who see you as competition and chase the smaller males away. The yelp sound imitates a female and will attract the males to you without chasing any away. The cluck sound is the most well-known sound—plus the easiest to perform—and will attract both genders.

BULLFROG

Bullfrogs can be hunted by day or by night, depending on your state or province's regulations. Different people have different ways to hunt bullfrogs, so you will have to pick your preferred method. Stalking a bullfrog by day is relatively easy, as they can be spotted resting on the banks of their watery home or have the top of their heads—with their huge eyes—just above the water looking at you. If you cannot see the bullfrogs, then listen for their croaks. You can scan the water with a flashlight or headlamp at night, and you will notice the eyes. By the eyes' size, you can judge the size of the frog and distinguish it from other animals such as alligators.

If you plan to hunt with a gun, aim for the head and watch where the body lands, as the frogs will be knocked back by the blast. This can cause you to lose your meal if you lose sight of it in the water. Most states/provinces don't allow for hunting with guns at night, so be sure to check the regulations before going frogging.

Many hunters also like to catch frogs by hand, but this can cause a considerable disturbance in the water and can cause several other frogs to flee from you. This, however, could still be a fun way to hunt and teach younger hunters how to catch a meal with no equipment. Then, there is the art of gigging. A gig is a pronged spear which is a well known method of hunting frogs. This spear can be thrust into the body of the frog either from a boat or as you stalk them through the water. Be sure to aim for the head where possible for an ethical shot. If you like the idea of fishing, you can also try to hook a frog. Tying a red piece of fabric around the hook and dangling it around the frog will cause it to try to eat it as the fabric mimics the appearance of an insect.

If you are hunting these animals at night, be sure not to cross in front of the light you are shining on them, as this will spook them. Once scared, they will hop into the water and be gone within seconds. You may find that you will need waders to truly enjoy hunting bullfrogs.

SNAPPING TURTLE

Avoid the head and go for the tail! This cannot be stressed enough, as their beak will take a finger if you are not careful. Once you have located a snapping turtle pond or habitat, there are many ways to get them out. If you are fearless, you can dive into the water with snorkeling gear and pick them out of the mud to place them in a boat. Also, you can set up traps that have a one-way opening. These traps are usually made of chicken wire and measure at about two feet in width and height with four feet in length. The bait—usually a meat source—should be placed at the back of the trap to entice the turtle through the trap entrance that won't allow it out. The trap needs to be anchored to the shore very firmly—with part of it sticking out of the water—as a trapped turtle is likely to struggle. If your state/province allows trapping, ensure that you are checking this daily to prevent a loss of your prey.

You can also try to hook these ancient beasts if you have the strength to do so. You will need a turtle hook—baited with some meat—and some thick cord that needs to be tied securely to the hook, as well as a big jug or similar floating device. This floating device also needs to be tied to something that will prevent it from floating away once the turtle has taken the bait. You can leave this device up overnight if you wish. You do not want to use a fishing line, as trying to pull the turtle up will cause the line to bite into your hands. Ideally, the turtle will go for the bait, take the hook, and then swim back down because of the floating device. Turtles will usually head toward land if they cannot swim back down into the mud. You should then easily be able to find the turtle when you return in the morning. Once you have the turtle, you will need to catch it physically. The beak needs to be occupied while you aim to grab the tail. Some people will end the kill immediately by shooting the turtle—or otherwise removing the head—while others prefer to keep the turtle alive for a few days to clean it in some fresh water and continue to feed it fresh meat or plant matter until you are ready to harvest it.

These animals prefer to feed at night and can be noted in the water by their heads and eyes that stick out of it. Look along the mud banks and fallen trees close to water to see signs that these animals are in the vicinity you are hunting.

CHAPTER 7

PRACTICE MAKES A MASTER

Simply having all this knowledge at your fingertips—or even in your brain—is not enough. You need to put into practice what you have been taught so far. You can't hope to get a perfect heart shot if you have never pulled a trigger in the past. Do you know how to clear a jammed weapon? How to set a snare? Not yet. Practicing the skills taught to you so far will mean the difference between a perfect, well-executed shot and a lost opportunity. Ensure that you are practicing correctly so that you are as close to perfect as possible. Each hunter does develop their way of doing things, but that doesn't mean that you are doing something wrong. Start with the basics, practice, and keep practicing those skills until they are second nature to you.

HOW TO BE A BETTER HUNTER

Hunting is a physical sport, and you will need to be fit to go for larger and larger game. Carrying a few squirrels home doesn't seem like much, but when you eventually bag a deer, you will have to take that back to your car, and deer are heavy! An excellent point to start before hunting is to get your body ready for extended walking with a weight. Taking an extended hike with your fully packed backpack is a way to build up your endurance and fitness. Start small and slowly build up the distance.

Learn to pack your gear correctly so that you are never overloaded in a hunt. Create a checklist to ensure that you have all the vital tools necessary for a hunt. Once you have this ready to go, pack the bag and see how it feels. Too heavy? See how you can rearrange items and what you can carry on yourself instead of in your bag. Perhaps some items can be combined to lessen the space taken up, such as wrapping duct tape around other items instead of just chucking a roll into your bag.

Take a few first aid courses and get certified to know how to handle any situation you may find yourself in. Practice on people—who are hopefully not injured—to gain confidence in your skills. Even if you don't get certified, be sure to know how to use all the items in your first aid kit, and learn how to build one yourself instead of relying on a standard kit you just buy.

When you are on these hikes, take the time to look for tracks and signs of animals in the vicinity. This gives you ample opportunity to study tracks and learn to identify the animals in your region. If you are not yet familiar with the tracks, take a book about tracks with you so that you can learn as you go. A great place to look for clear tracks is in the mud close to riverbanks.

Consider camping overnight so that you can test your wilderness skills, such as making a fire from scratch or creating a shelter from the resources around you. Do check the rules and regulations of the park you wish to camp in, and follow all their safety guides to ensure that you remain safe while doing this. If you are planning on fishing or trying your hand at hunting small game on this trip, ensure that you have the necessary licenses to do this without getting possible fines. Take the time to scout while you are hiking. The more information you gather about the location you are in, the better.

The quality of your equipment is something you need to consider. Although you do not need the top-of-the-line merchandise for hunting, you need to be able to weed out poor-quality goods by testing them rigorously. Learn how to repair equipment that could break, and keep your gear in good working order. Even if you are not hunting, always be prepared. Quality gear is pricey, so start with the slightly cheaper gear and save toward the more expensive if this will become a hobby you intend to keep doing every year. If something new comes out—and it is affordable—test it out to see if it measures up to what you expect of it. Never buy something that looks cool but has no actual function, as it will only weigh you down.

Don't stick to only one type of weapon. Branching out and using multiple hunting tools allows you to sharpen various skills that can impact which tools you use. Using a slingshot will enable you to hone your stalking skills which will, in turn, make it easier to sneak up on the larger game when you use your rifle. Knowing how to use different weapons can also extend your hunting season, as you can easily switch from hunting with a rifle, a shotgun, or even a muzzleloader. Clean your tools! This isn't just your guns but also your knives. Keep barrels clean and clear and knives free of blood. Dirty equipment lowers their durability and their functionality.

Use any and every possible resource you can to get better, whether that is going to the range to practice with a weapon or scouring the forums for people to help you with questions. Read books, speak to people, and even go on hunts with other veteran hunters to gain vital experience without having to pull the trigger. If you do pull that trigger and miss, don't think of it as a failure. Think of it as a learning opportunity. When you miss a shot, think about what went wrong and how you can correct it for the next time you can line up a shot. Not all hunts end with an animal in the bag. Learn to accept this.

If you do succeed in a hunt, learn how to do it ethically. An ethical shot is a clean shot that puts an animal down quickly and with little to no pain. Better for it and better for the meat left behind. Practice how to skin and gut (dress) an animal after it has been shot so that you harvest what is needed without losing any of the good parts. With larger animals, there are many ways to dress them—such as gutless versus retaining gut while dressing—so practice which suits you better. Take a friend. The easiest way to learn is through teaching, and we know that two heads are better than one.

Lastly, treat the land and animals with respect. Do not take potshots at animals. Aim for a clean shot that prevents injury. Pick up your trash and dispose of it properly. This includes guts, packaging, and other possible waste. If you meet other hunters, you can swap stories, but you shouldn't hunt their area. Common courtesy will see you making friends with people who are willing to share their tips and tricks of the trade.

SHARPENING SPECIFIC SKILLS

Some skills need to be perfected over time and are something that needs to be practiced. Something like turkey and duck calls need to be perfected to get the animals to come to you, and you need to get good at this to improve your hunting chances. Other skills, such as learning how to set a snare, won't just enhance your arsenal of taking an animal—it may someday save your life when you have no other choice.

Bird Calls

When making use of bird calls, it isn't just about making a sound but how you make the sound. Each call is different and means different things to the birds. By practicing with the call, you can imitate a welcoming call, a mating call, or a feeding call, all of which the wild animals will listen for and decide whether they want to be enticed or not. Speak to veteran hunters of these animals to learn how they use the respective calls to attract potential prey and learn from them.

Don't know anyone who is an expert? Simply look online where videos are posted that teach you how to make the calls with various types of equipment. Once you have the basics down, you can practice out in nature. However, be wary of where you practice, as turkeys have a great capacity to learn. You can inadvertently teach them how to avoid hunters in the future.

When practicing your turkey calls, go to an area where no hunting is allowed. You can communicate with these animals using the yelps, purrs, and a variety of other sounds. If you are consistently getting replies—whether from humans or other turkeys—you are doing something right. This is something that takes a while to perfect, so keep at it with the various tools that are available for this.

Making Snares

Unless you are in a situation where you need to survive, ensure that snare usage is legal before using them. Practicing making them is not illegal, so take the time to get familiar with the basic setup of the common snare. To make the snare, you will need a picture hanging wire or snare wire and something to cut the wire—some people like to use a 24-gauge steel wire, but the preference is up to you.

Cut about an 18 inch to a two-foot piece of wire loose from the spool. At the one end of the wire, create a loop— about the size of your thumb pad—and then twist it around the wire, allowing it to get smaller and smaller until you have twisted enough so that it won't unravel.

This is called a slip loop, and you now have to feed the other end of the wire through it to make the noose. You can then decide to leave the other end open or to create a larger slip loop to be used as an anchor point that you can drive a stake through. If you leave it untied, then you can tie it to an anchor when you are ready to do so.

The size of the noose will depend on the animal that you are hunting. If you are hunting rabbits or hares, then the noose size should be the size of your fist. Any smaller and the rabbit will just move it aside, and any larger can cause it to hop through or have its back legs caught instead of its neck. This can lead the animal to suffer when caught, which needs to be avoided. If you are hunting squirrels, you will need to make it smaller, or the prey will simply just hop through it.

Making a snare is the easy part. Anyone can do it, and the skill comes in knowing where to place the snare to be most effective.

Setting Snares

For a snare to be accurate, you need to know how your prey thinks and where it likes to move. By knowing that, you will be able to set the snare so that the prey will head toward it without knowing it is there, as you are using the natural runs that the animals use. Scout the area to see where these animals are moving from cover to cover, and set the snare in its path where a natural tunnel is formed. Th e snares will need to be anchored to something that cannot be uprooted, as you want the animal to be caught and not run away with the trap attached to it.

Once the snare is set—a little off the ground—then look to prevent the animal from simply going around it. Prey are very clever, more than we give them credit for. Any open spaces around the snare need to be eliminated. You can do this by putting sticks in the ground or snow so that gaps are closed, and the only way for the animal to get through to their hiding area is to go through the space where the snare is set. If you want to prevent the animal from jumping over the snare, you may need to put a branch in the way. Leave the snare for several hours while you set up a few more.

If a snare hasn't caught something in a few days, you will need to read the tracks to see why this is so. There could be a gap that the animal has gone through your funnel, or they have jumped over or simply moved the snare out of the way. You must adjust to the animal's intelligence. Sometimes you may find a still-living animal in the snare, and you will need to dispatch it as ethically and quickly as possible. Do not try to remove the snare from a living animal, as they will do everything in their power to escape, including biting and kicking.

Another type of snare you can make use of is the spring snare. To set this snare, you will need a sapling that you can bend over that is close to the animal's run, two pieces of wood (one longer than the other) that can be connected to each other through a notch close to the ends, your prepared wire snare, and another piece of wire that will be connecting the tree to your trap. You can drive the longer of the two pieces of wood into the ground next to the run. This is your anchor point for the trap. Tie the spare wire to the bent-over sapling and connect the smaller notched pieces of wood. Attach the snare to this piece of wood as well before setting the trap by placing the two notched pieces of wood together. The wire connected to the tree needs to be taut but not so taut that it rips the anchor point out. Once the trap is correctly set up, make sure that the snare stays open over the run. You can achieve this by adding a few smaller and weaker sticks to keep it open. You can also create a funneling effect that was used with the regular snare, but it must not interfere with the trap's ability to be sprung when the animal gets snared. Instead of the animal remaining trapped on the ground to be picked off by predators, this trap, once sprung, hoists the animal into the air to keep it out of reach of most predators. With this kind of trap, you can notice if it has been triggered or not from a distance and can therefore prevent you from checking the area too frequently and scaring off potential prey.

(Tip: Once a snare has done its purpose, please remove it from the area to not catch unfortunate animals that you will not use.)

Making and Setting a Deadfall Trap

There are several deadfall traps that you can make use of. Some are simpler in design, while others are more complex. For this book, we will be looking at the Paiute deadfall trap. To make this trap, you need several components, which are the large flat rock, a short vertical post stick, string or cord, the longer angle stick, the trigger component, stick for the trigger (sticks need to be as straight as possible), and some bait the rodent of choice may like (berries, nuts, or seeds). The angle and vertical sticks should be the thickness of your thumb, but this will depend on the weight of the rock you are using. If the rock causes these sticks to bow under the weight, then you will need stronger sticks. The trigger stick needs to be thinner than the vertical and angle sticks but strong enough to hold the trap without setting it off. The string can be made of cotton or a fishing line, but alternatively, you can also braid plant matter together to create a cord if you have none.

Find a sturdy, straight stick to create your vertical post and angle stick. Cut the vertical stick to have a pointed end (V-shape) at the top and a flat lower end. Now, cut a longer section of the main stick which also ends in a V-shape. Close to this end, cut a notch so that the vertical post stick can fit in it. The angled stick will be supporting the rock and not the vertical post. Next, make the trigger component. This is a thin piece of flat wood (about two inches by one inch) with a hole drilled through one end. The cord goes through this hole and can be knotted in place, or a loop can be created, which can be held in place by a smaller stick through the loop end. The other end of the cord is then tied to the end of the angled stick You can notch the bottom of this stick to help with keeping the cord attached. Where the cord will wrap around the bottom of the vertical stick, make a notch so that the cord doesn't slip along the stick's length.

Now that all your components are prepped and ready, you can start setting the trap. It may take some practice trying to balance everything and getting the correct lengths to correspond to the weight of the rock, so practice it while you are not in a survival situation. Balance the angled stick on the vertical stick using the notch. Place the rock's edge on the angled stick, making sure the middle edge is over both sticks for balance. Wrap the trigger mechanism around the notch in the vertical post and set the trap by placing the trigger stick against the trigger and the rock and an angle that the trap isn't sprung. When built correctly, the trap should stand by itself, with the angled stick and trigger stick balancing the rock precariously. Once balanced, add some bait on one side of the trigger stick and then leave the trap to do its job.

Rodents are very clever and will sometimes take the bait without setting off the trap. If this happens frequently, you may have to use a thinner trigger stick or change its angle for it to be more sensitive. The Paiute deadfall trap can be made larger if you want to catch animals such as squirrels and rabbits. However, snares are likely best for them to conserve the meat better than a deadfall trap. Deadfall traps are perfect for small game animals that can be used to bait larger traps or hooks for fishing.

Shooting Practice

Whichever weapon you are making use of, you will need to practice with it—not a few days before the hunt but constantly. Keeping your skills sharp is the difference between a meal or going hungry when you should be trying to survive. Even if you aren't in survival mode, keeping your skills honed is something every hunter should do regardless of year.

Some people like to put hours into a range of some sort, and this does have its merits, but it isn't ideal. A range offers a straight shot with only distance as your challenge, and it is not enough when your prey is a moving target. You will need to practice your hunting skills under various conditions such as rain, snow, and wind to get accustomed to what could happen in reality when you are on a hunt. Take care when practicing in your backyard for archery or using a slingshot to ensure that you do not harm anyone around you. Set up targets like tin cans on a string to simulate a moving target. Suppose you have a larger, more rural property. In that case, you can set up 3D animal targets in the brush, on hills, down a hill, any place conceivable to allow you the opportunity to practice difficult shots and stalking.

Practice the way you take your shots. If you mostly shoot standing, then practice shooting from a seated position and vice versa until you can do both. You can even consider shooting on the move to see if this is a skill you can sharpen, though always be sure that your shots are ethical at all times, even against targets. Suppose you practice just to hit the edge of a target. In that case, when it comes to shooting a living animal, it can mean the possibility of a complete miss or an injured animal fleeing in panic and pain to succumb to its wounds much later where you cannot get to it.

Work on your weaknesses until they are your strengths, and learn to leave a shot unfired. One of the most important aspects of hunting is knowing that your shot will find its mark. If you are not sure, you will need to move into a different position to get a better shot or allow the animal to move away. Always aim for a quick and clean kill.

CHAPTER 8

DOMINATE YOUR FIRST HUNT

Before you go out and buy what you think you need to have a successful hunt, consider the order of things you need to do. The first isn't going out to get a gun; though this is an exciting purchase, it really shouldn't be your first. There are many steps to take before setting out for a hunt, so be sure to follow them closely to allow you to get the most from your experience.

PREPARING BEFORE THE HUNT

Before you can even begin to think about hunting, you need to complete your Hunter Ed regardless of whether your state or province requires it or not. By completing this, you will be certified to hunt safely with whatever weapon you choose in whatever state/province you want. If you are new to hunting, you may never have handled a hunting tool before, so it is a good idea to use mentorship programs that can be found in your state/province. The programs allow you to learn from veteran hunters and people who are masters in a specific aspect of hunting. These people can teach you to hunt with different kinds of guns, bows, and other weapons. Not only that, but they are the ones that will invite you on hunts so that you can see one in action without having the pressure of bringing a prize home. By working with a mentor, you learn the necessities of hunting with others, sharing, and respecting the land you are making use of.

Mentors can also share information about their favorite equipment they use to bring their prizes home. They can show you how to do proper field dressing and cleaning of the animal so that you take the best parts of your hard work home. These tips and tricks of the trade cannot be learned in a book but only at the feet of masters, so listen to what they have to say because you have a lot to learn. By being in a mentorship program, you can even pick up a hunting buddy that will make the larger hunts a lot easier to deal with in the future. Once you become a master, think of giving back to the community by teaching young ones the skills you learned and were introduced to. This is how you can keep the tradition of hunting alive.

Many people like to hunt alone, but that doesn't mean that they aren't willing to share information they have gathered over the years. Take the time to join conservation groups and participate in their activities, such as volunteering for cleanup days. Though this doesn't seem appealing to most people, it is a great way for you to come together and speak with like-minded people. From people in these groups, you will be able to gain local information about farmers who are willing to let hunters onto their land, the best spots for hunting certain animals, and even get exposed to people who are eager to teach you more about scouting or tracking.

The biggest asset to a hunter isn't their gear or weapon—it is information. Gather as much knowledge as possible from various sources so that you can form a clear image of what you want from a hunt. Know which hunting seasons lead into another season so that you can combine hunting for one animal while scouting for another. Teach yourself about edible items out in the wild that can be found in the state/province you want to hunt in. With this knowledge, you will live off the land even if you do not harvest from a hunt.

Learn about your state or province's regulations about hunting, get licensed, and then get started on preparing to hunt small game animals. Now is the time to look at the gear and clothing you may need for a hunt. With the knowledge from this book and anything extra from mentors, you will know exactly what is needed in your pack when hunting for certain animals. Purchase what you need, and test it at home before taking it out into the wilderness. Make sure the clothing you get is suited to the weather and regulations of the state/province you are hunting in. Practice with different weapons to see which feels best to use for the animal you want to hunt. Put the hours into learning how to use, clean, and maintain the weapon. Consider learning to use both a firearm and another weapon that isn't a firearm so that you can have access to different game and seasons that you can hunt in. Keep those shooting skills sharp by practicing a few days out of the week during the off-season.

Scout the areas where you will be hunting both digitally and physically, having your boots on the ground. Take the time to look for the tracks in the area, and note possible feeding areas where the animal of choice is likely to show up. Look for places where you could approach from with and without cover. While scouting, you can even make use of practicing your stalking of animals in the region. See how close you can get without alerting the animals.

PREPARING YOURSELF FOR A HUNT

If you want a good hunt, you need to be in great shape to go after prey in a variety of conditions. You will need to get fit and break in your hunting boots and gear. Very few people have the fitness for hiking miles with a fully packed backpack, so start small. Go for a short walk along the flat ground with your new hiking boots so that you can slowly break them in. Then, once they are more comfortable, start stacking those miles on them. Once you can comfortably walk for several miles on flat ground, take up hiking to help you build the endurance for more challenging terrain that will await you on a hunt. Set goals for the distance you want to reach, and when you get those goals successfully time and time again, it is time to start doing the hikes with your hunting gear. Try doing these hikes under various conditions to get the feel of what it will be like when you are on an actual hunt.

However, hunting isn't just about the physical strength of a person but also their mentality. Hunting small game is easier to carry home, but when you are bagging a larger game that requires multiple trips in and out of where you shot it, the brain needs to take over for those tired legs. You need to be mentally strong to handle the weight and the distance to ensure that you bring the whole harvest back home. Hunting takes you out of your comfort zone, so be prepared for sore feet, feeling wet and cold, and possibly being hungry. There is no such thing as an easy hunt. Even if you have one easy hunt, you are likely never to have something like that again.

Hunting can be an emotional roller coaster for some people as well. People who pride themselves as animal lovers struggle with the concept of hunting sometimes, and it does make it difficult for them to enjoy this practice. To overcome this aspect, you will have to go into the hunt with a clear goal of what you want to achieve. This will help you to visualize what you want from a hunt. Remember, you do not have to take the shot if you don't want to or need to. Finding your quarry is just as big a rush as taking it. Please make your choice, and then follow through with it.

PREPARING THE HUNT

By hunting small game, you are guaranteed the possibility of a hunt, as more people are likely competing for the larger game instead of rabbits. Enjoy the fact that you will hunt mostly undisturbed by other hunters. Even the gear required to hunt the smaller animals is cheaper than those required for the larger game. Start by choosing an animal you want to hunt, then check for the various licenses, permits, and other necessities you may need. You won't need a duck call if you are hunting rabbits.

Ensure that the sights—if you are using them—are set and ready to be used. Then, go through your gear and attire to make sure everything is ready to be packed. Only take what is needed so that you do not become encumbered. Come up with a plan on how you see the hunt will go. This will allow you to remain focused on the hunt when it happens and not second-guess yourself about certain decisions. Stick to this plan unless an emergency occurs. Know the limits of your license and the limit of the range you are allowed to hunt on. Suppose you notice that there is a chance of stepping onto private property—phone the owner to get permission.

Hunting starts as soon as you wake on the day of the hunt. Take note of the weather, and consider which animals will be out and about. Once you decide to continue with the day, you need to keep your eyes and ears open to find the prey you want. When an animal is spotted, consider which is the best way to get closer. Play on the animal's nature to help you decide on this. Nervous animals will flush out with a stop-and-go method while animals eating calmly in the distance can be stalked. Patience is more than just a virtue, and it is the lifeblood of a hunter. If you do not have the patience to sit quietly or to stalk prey, then it is best you learn or find another hobby to keep yourself occupied.

When you eventually have that animal lined up in your sight, take the time to ask yourself a few questions. Can I get closer to get a better shot without disturbing the animal? Will this be an ethical shot? Is it safe to fire my weapon? Once you are sure the shot will be ethical, then take it and bag your prize. This is about the quality of your shot, not the quantity. You would rather have three prized rabbits taken with three good shots than three rabbits on you and the fourth suffering in its warren until it expires with a poor fourth shot.

Remain safe at all times. This means being aware of potential dangers in the wilderness, such as other hunters and predators, as well as letting people know about where you are. By ensuring that there are people who know where you are, how long you will be gone, and when you will return, you guarantee that if you cannot get back (for whatever reason), there will be help arriving quickly.

GOING BIGGER

When hunting small game, you can sharpen your skills and build up confidence with each animal you take successfully. However, once your confidence is up, don't fear failure. It is just another learning opportunity that all adds up to a larger hunt. While you are practicing on the small game, see if you can get some tags for larger animals. Getting tags and licenses for areas that are not your own can take some time to do well ahead of the season you want to hunt so doing it this way, you will have the time to prepare when you get those tags. Don't be disappointed if you don't get the tags for the animal you want to hunt, as there are general hunting licenses that still allow you to hunt other animals.

Hunting larger animals comes with more difficulties. They are wary of humans, and you will need to mask your scent to prevent them from noticing you. You will also need to be significantly fitter and stronger to take on these hunts. You will have to walk vast distances and carry any harvested items back with you. Squirrels do not weigh much, but a hind quarter of an elk will be a chore.

It would be best to be wary of the potential diseases that a state/province has that will prevent you from taking certain parts of an animal back with you. There are several states/provinces where animals have become infected with the chronic wasting disease (CWD), which is highly contagious. Get more information about this disease to ensure that you are allowed to keep what you harvest instead of having to waste it. Make contact with the state or province's Fish and Wildlife Service Department to get more information about what to do if you come across an animal with this disease. It is also a good idea to keep an eye out for diseases that can affect you! If there is Lyme disease in the area, ensure you have taken all the precautions necessary to prevent infection from tick bites.

CONCLUSION

This book aims to instill the knowledge of hunting the smaller game available to anyone who wishes to explore the beauty of the American wilderness. Although it isn't an easy task, and you will need to spend some time training your body, this is a sport that anyone can do: man, woman, or child. Hunting is more than just that photograph of you holding your very first prize. It is about accumulating knowledge, being prepared, and knowing how to apply everything you have learned.

The starting point for all new hunters is to take the time to get the Hunter Ed before gathering everything you will need to go out into the wilderness to gain invaluable experience. Whether you are scouting from the air or taking the time to break in some boots with the family on a hike, keep an eye out for hunting locations that will yield the prizes you want from nature. Know your limitations regarding weapons and terrain that you can manage on your first hunt to ensure you get the most from every hunt.

Become familiar with the laws and regulations in your state/province for weapons—as well as snares and traps—as this will ensure that you will not be fined under the guise of "Oh, I didn't know!" As a responsible hunter, you have to ensure that you know the rules. Make an effort to get to know what kind of equipment you will need to have on the hunt, then ask on hunter forums for the opinions of others on the merchandise. Scour the Internet for videos of other people's hunts to learn some tips that you can try to apply to your hunt. A great place to meet like-minded people that enjoy hunting is a Facebook group called, "Hunting for Greatness Community," a community that shares a ton of valuable information about hunting for beginners and veterans alike. Once a member, you will find friendly people who are always willing to help you out with any of your hunting queries.

Ensure that any equipment you intend to use is thoroughly tested before taking it out into the wild, as this is a surefire way to get into trouble if you don't. Practice with any weapons that you will be using, as that is the only way you will improve your skill and establish the quickest and cleanest way to dispatch your prey. Learn the difference between a potential sloppy shot versus a clean kill. Patience is needed on a hunt, but that isn't the only skill you will need. Depending on the weapon of choice, you may have to make use of various stalking and hunting techniques while all the time asking yourself if you are in the correct position to claim a prize or if it is best to watch it move along.

As much as we all hope for a perfect hunt, sometimes disaster can strike, but it doesn't have to remain a disaster if you are fully prepared. By having a personally packed first aid kit, you ensure your safety and your possible survival. By preparing for the worst, you will always be ready for everything. Knowing how to build a shelter, get water, start a fire, and obtain different food sources, you will keep yourself living long enough until professional help can make its way to you.

To efficiently hunt your quarry, you need to understand what it needs from its environment in terms of food and shelter. Once you understand this, you will effortlessly find tracks and signs of where they have been. Keep within your tags and licenses within the scope, as this is what sets a true hunter apart from poachers. To avoid being labeled as a poacher at all times, know where you are so that you are not hunting on property that doesn't allow hunting or is privately owned.

No one is just born a great hunter, so take the time to practice everything you have learned in this book, as it will come in handy one day. Know the tracks. Know the habits. Know the boundaries. Become a better hunter by learning from others and teaching those that ask you questions as you improve at bringing back prized harvests again and again. By starting small, you will gain the confidence to eventually build your hunts up to go after the giants of America: moose, bear, and wolves.

Now that you have read this book from cover to cover, you are ready to go forth and prepare yourself for the great outdoors. No longer will you have to stare longingly at the mountains and feel the jealousy of someone who has a freezer full of fresh meat from a hunt. That can be you. That can be anyone willing to try hunting. Get yourself educated, certified, then gather all the equipment you need, and set forth on your hunting adventure. Nothing is holding you back. Remember, we hunt to live and live to hunt!

EAT MY MEAT

A BEGINNERS FIELD DRESSING GUIDE FOR SMALL GAME

INTRODUCTION

Hunting can be incredibly satisfying when you're experienced. You get the thrill of the hunt, followed by the immense satisfaction that you've been able to catch something that is going to provide sustenance for you and your family. While we rarely eat the skins of our catches, they can be useful for other purposes. However, if you've never hunted and dressed your kills, you might feel entirely overwhelmed by the prospect of doing so. You may feel lost, confused, and may even make some mistakes that will render your kill inedible. Of course, to dress a kill in the field will require practice that you can only get in a hands-on environment.

I was born in Northern Ontario. My home was surrounded by thick forest and marshes that were ripe with many animals for the taking. Ever since the tender age of three, I've been taught the basics of hunting. I grew up raised by wolves—or at least, it felt like it with my siblings running wild. I began with a little slingshot, shooting at snakes, partridge, and any other small game I could land a hit on. Hunting flows through my blood.

I've spent over 20 years out in nature, learning what the beautiful Mother Earth offers us. Sure, I could live in a city, surrounded by everything I need just a few clicks of the internet away, but is that living? I don't think so. For me, true happiness is the exhilaration of providing for myself. It is to be out in nature and see that we all are interconnected. We hunt, we eat, we live. Animals are born, they die, they return to the earth. The circle of life might make some uncomfortable, but to me, it makes every moment of living that much more desirable. It makes every moment of my life feel like an adventure, truly cherished because you never know what day will be your last.

Over the years, I've had plenty of time to learn about hunting and field dressing my meat. I've practiced and perfected my technique. And now, it's time that I take my expertise and pass it on to the next generation. Hunting is a sport that everyone should learn to appreciate—after all, not too long ago, our ancestors had to go out and kill their food on their own. Grocery stores don't exist in the state of nature. Be self-sufficient to survive in a natural world, and that's where hunting and dressing come into play.

You might be surprised to discover that hunting isn't necessarily the hardest part of the process. To kill an animal is relatively easy. However, to clean it and prepare it for consumption takes much more finesse than simply shooting something. As you read through my guide, you're going to be introduced to information that will help you become a professional field dresser. This is the information that I wish I had when I first began hunting—it would have saved me from wasting time and valuable meat.

Nowadays, I love field dressing, but I also understand that so many people are squeamish about the entire process. That's why I've made this guide as easy to follow as possible for beginners: This is supposed to be the beginner's holy grail about everything that you need to know before you ever step foot out into the wilderness. By the end of this, you'll have the technical knowledge—then, all you're missing is the practice to master it.

If you're unsure what I mean about field dressing, don't worry too much about it. Simply put, field dressing involves removing the animal's internal organs to avoid decay and improve the general quality of the meat. It comes with several critical benefits that will help you ensure that you stay healthy when eating meat that isn't prepared professionally.

1. Preventing bacterial growth: It helps you avoid the growth of bacteria on the carcass, therefore ensuring that the meat stays fresh until it is adequately preserved. If the meat is left without field dressing, it can decay quickly. The act of field dressing helps cool the meat, lowering the body temperature of the meat to prevent it from remaining in the danger zone too long.

2. Ease of transportation: Field dressing makes it very easy to move your game from the field to your home because you've already removed the guts and other parts of the animal that you will not be using or consuming. Especially for larger game, such as deer, this could be the difference between carrying it or not.

3. It gets you the full hunter's experience: Your hunting experience is incomplete if you have not dressed the animal yourself. You will enjoy the whole experience when you field dress an animal you hunted. This allows you to understand the completeness of the process and to have all credit for the meat.

As you read this book, you'll discover the most critical aspects of dressing and field dressing for minor games. It assumes that you're a total novice to field dressing and that everything you'll be learning is brand new. We'll be covering several popular small game animals that can be found in North America.

If you are just like me that have a knack for small game, then know that I put this material together with you in mind to make it easy for you to handle your small game meat. Hunting is what I do and love. After studying this field guide, easily field dress your small game, butcher it and package it later. You can expect to find information such as:

- How to carry out field dressing
- Steps to take to the field to help you dress small game animals are explicitly found in North America.
- Effective transporting techniques to take your small game home in such a way that the meat maintains its freshness and quality.
- How to Hang, cool, and age your meat for the best tasting.
- How to butcher your meat and butchering methods.
- Cooking your small game and secret recipes.

Are you ready to prepare yourself for the next step in becoming self sufficient? There's no better time than the present to get started. Why wait one day longer? Be ready to process your next kill. It's not as hard as so many people make it out to be once you've tried.

1

BASIC GEAR, TOOLS, AND EQUIPMENT FOR BEGINNERS

Before you rush out to hunt with just your weapon of choice, consider that there are many, many pieces of equipment that you probably want to have on hand. This will vary from whether you wish to hunt small game small or big game. You'll need to kill, process, and store your game, and you'll also need some general safety supplies on hand just in case you need them.

Your tools are essential to your success as you hunt and field dress the game you have. You need to be prepared to keep yourself comfortable as well. Finding the fine line between having everything you're going to need and being able to carry it all can be a bit of a balancing act, but the more you work on finding that perfect combination of what you should have on hand and what you should do while out and about.

ESSENTIAL STORAGE AND TRANSPORTATION EQUIPMENT

Going to the field without the right equipment is a waste of your time. You want to be sure that you are prepared to execute a clean and proper field dressing, so you don't kill your game in vain and so you can ensure that you are safe throughout the process. Many diseases could pass from animal to hunter during your interaction with wild game, and many steps could pose a challenge if you try to prepare your game without all the proper supplies.

BACKPACK

An essential item that helps you to keep everything else organized. Your backpack serves as your one-stop shop for everything that you'll need during your time hunting. It should be large enough that you're able to fit everything you'll need, but also not too large or heavy, so it doesn't impede your movement as you hunt. If you're not interested in a backpack, using even a game vest or fanny pack can also provide you with a valid option. As long as it fits all of your supplies and tools, any sort of storage will work.

GAME BAGS

If you want to keep your meat clean, one of the best ways to do so is to ensure that you've got a game bag. You can put your meat right into the game bag before you take the meat to the butcher elsewhere, or you can also put dressed animals right into the bag to prevent maggots from flies landing on the meat, as well as to cool the meat. Game bags are breathable enough to let the remnants of body heat escape without letting in bugs. These come in many materials, such as cotton, synthetic, or even trash bags. Plastic bags can be used in a pinch, but the meat won't breathe unless you leave it open, which leads to problems with bugs contaminating the meat.

TRASH BAGS

If you've got a lot of waste that you don't want to leave out in the wild for Mother Nature to take care of, you can always pack along a trash bag for all of your garbage. In a pinch, a trash bag has a lot of great purposes, from being able to create a barrier between your meat and the ground while you field dress it, to being a rain jacket if a sudden storm passes by, and even used as a game bag in a pinch, though this is usually not recommended.

HARNESS AND SLED

If you intend to kill many animals at once, you might also consider getting yourself a sled and harness. Keeping a harness in your toolbox when going hunting will make it easy for you to come back with less frustration after a day out in the fields. If you would have to drag your hunt to your car, you will need to use a harness to distribute the weight of the animals evenly on you so that you can carry it easily. A sled could also help you transport your meat after field dressing in a snowy part of town.

☰ ICE CHEST

If you can do so, it's a good idea to have an ice chest accessible during your hunting trip. Whether you set up a camp or have a home base set up in your car, knowing that you have ice means that you don't have to rush home as soon as you get the kill. You can leave your processed game to chill while you continue to hunt. Chilling the meat is essential to prevent it from spoiling too quickly.

☰ ESSENTIAL FIELD DRESSING, SKINNING, AND BUTCHERING EQUIPMENT

When it's time for you to skin, field dress, and butcher your game, you'll want to go into it with several supplies that you'll be able to use to make the process easier. While you could probably get by with any old knife and your hands sometimes, you'll probably want to have some equipment on hand so you can get through the process easier and keep things cleaner. Remember, cleanliness is essential if you're going to eat the food you've hunted with a low risk of illness. Keeping the meat clean is often the best prevention, and that cleanliness starts in butchering your meat the right way.

☰ BOWL

Before you begin, an important consideration is to ensure that you have some sort of bowl and container that you can use for the meat. Since we're talking about small game here, be able to take a plain stainless steel bowl that will fit just fine for all but the largest game. This prevents you from placing your kill on the ground while opening it up to remove the entrails.

GLOVES

It's important to use gloves for your field dressing for sanitary purposes. The gloves should be elbow length so that it shields your arms from any contamination. Try to sanitize your hands before putting on your gloves, and if you're frequently in areas where water access is difficult, consider getting disposable gloves. I prefer using gloves made from latex material or one with a latex feel for better grip and fitting.

SHARP KNIVES

A sharp knife is an essential tool for field dressing; you'll want at least two of them, with one heavier and the other smaller to cut through delicate organs. You may even want to consider keeping a small sharpener with you if any of your knives aren't up to par with what you'd like.

BONE SAW

Depending on what you're hunting, carry a bone saw as well. This will make it easier to cut through tough bones, especially if you get ambitious and go for a deer if the opportunity arises. This shouldn't be a problem for most small game, but if you have a large rabbit or goose, you might use one if you can't quite get the leverage. It could be good just in case, too. It's always better to be prepared, and these aren't too heavy.

☰ HEADLAMP

Just in case it isn't one of those lucky days where you shoot an animal in the early hours. If the evening comes down on you while you are trying to field dress your meat, be well prepared by having your headlamp with you. You should get a headlamp with powerful battery life and designed for mountaineers so that it fits into your backpack and get one that is sturdy and can be firmly placed on the head, and even in cases of a slight fall it can work perfectly.

☰ CLEAN RAGS AND PAPER TOWELS

Messes happen in the best of times. This can be a huge problem when you're in the middle of the forest without access to clean running water. At the very least, you can use rags and paper towels to blot up the mess or perhaps pour a bit of your bottled water onto it to use as a sort of wet cloth. Try keeping these within a sealed plastic bag, so they stay nice and clean until you need them.

2

TRANSPORTATION AND STORAGE

After you've hunted and cleaned your harvest, you've done just half the work. Unless you're going to slap that meat onto a campfire and enjoy it nearly immediately, you must take the time to transport the meat appropriately. That meat, once processed, needs to be made into a cooler or refrigerator as soon as possible. This is especially true if you're hunting in the heat of summer. It may not be as important amid winter, depending upon where you are hunting and what the temperatures in the area are like, but it's a good idea to ensure that your meat is somewhere cool as soon as possible.

With small game, you're already at an advantage compared to people trying to bring home some other large harvest. You're lucky in the sense that the meat that you collect can be stored in a cooler or some other easily transported case that can help keep it cool.

The most important thing to remember is that if you're ever in doubt about whether your meat is safe to eat, it's better to dispose of it than risk eating it anyway to prevent the transmission of disease. However, there are many ways that you can take care of your harvests to keep them safe and ready to eat.

As you read through this chapter, you will be introduced to three important aspects of hunting. First, we'll address what to do to clean up your kill site. Then, we'll go over how to store the meat safely so you know you can enjoy it when you get home. Finally, we will discuss how to transport it home safely to be confident that you did nothing that might contaminate the meat.

≡ BEFORE YOU LEAVE THE KILL SITE

Upon killing small game, it's essential to get it cleaned as quickly as possible to prevent it from causing problems later on. The entrails swell up and may even burst within the animal's abdomen, which can cause you many issues. Alternatively, if you pierced the intestines or stomach, the leakage can cause the meat to spoil, and that spoilage can happen rapidly if the weather is warmer.

However, it's considered in poor taste to leave behind scraps. Most people don't care to find piles of entrails, scraps, and bones that you've left behind. Thankfully, with small game, the entrails are much smaller than if you had hunted, say, a deer, but you'll still need to dispose of them properly. Not doing so, especially if you're somewhere relatively popular for people to travel through, is a problem. You'll need to dispose of the waste appropriately. This is where cleaning the kill site comes in handy. You usually have a few options for this:

1. Take the entrails with you to dispose of at home
2. Bury the entrails,
3. Leave the entrails somewhere other animals can eat it

Taking the entrails home with you can annoy you most times because you have to carry them. This is where extra sealable baggies and trash bags will come in handy, as you can simply zip up the entrails into a bag to carry them, hopefully with no stench or mishaps, and then dispose of them in your trash when you finish your trip.

Burying the entrails is always a popular option, and you can do so simply by digging a deep trench, tossing the entrails in, and putting the dirt back on top. This will allow you to avoid dealing with the entrails as you transport your meat home, and no one will be disturbed by the waste left out. However, you'll need to make sure you don't choose a location near a body of water to bury them. Burying too close to a water source might contaminate it.

Leaving them out for other animals to eat is another option, but you need to be mindful of where you do. You will also need to check if this is even legal where hunting, like many hunting grounds, prohibit this behavior. If it is legal where you are hunting, you can do so safely by moving the entrails somewhere that other people aren't likely to find them and then burying them in a bit of leaf litter somewhere, allowing other animals like mice and foxes to come by and eat their fill. This is perhaps the easiest of the options but isn't available everywhere.

This means that there are also many things that you simply shouldn't do when disposing of your entrails. This includes:

1. Dumping them somewhere public.
2. Leaving them out in the open in areas people enjoy, such as hiking trails or in direct eyesight of a hiking trail.
3. Dumping them in or near water.
4. Leaving them on the side of the road.

Keep in mind that the land that you hunt on is likely also enjoyed by other people who want to go about their business without suddenly discovering a pile of half-decayed intestines lying on the side of the path. They want to know that they can enjoy the area as well. By making sure you dispose of your waste appropriately, you ensure that the public opinion of hunters isn't damaged, which could also restrict the ability that you have to hunt further in the future. You want to ensure that hunting is kept sacred. You don't want people to feel a need to petition to restrict hunting, so respect the other people who have a use for the land as well.

SAFE STORAGE

After your meat is cleaned, the next key aspect is getting it down to temperature as quickly as possible. Whether you're going to hang the meat or plan on just taking it home, you want it to be at or below 40 degrees Fahrenheit or 5 degrees celsius to ensure that it doesn't spoil. This can be difficult, depending on where and when you're hunting. Or, it may be easy to simply leave the kill hanging in a game bag from a tree branch if the temperatures are low enough.

If it's not cool enough outdoors for your meat, you'll need to store it in a cooler to reduce the risk of spoilage. However, you might use alternatives to the ice to keep it cool. While ice is cheap and effective, it also melts quickly into a wet mess, and moisture encourages spoilage. Many people will still use ice while making sure their meat is well-stored, such as plastic bags. However, you can also choose to put the meat in other containers, such as game bags. Instead of using ice, you could choose to use frozen water bottles. These will melt much slower, mainly if you use a good cooler.

My favorite cooler is, bar none, the Yeti cooler. However, these are expensive, and that price can be prohibitive for some hunters. A cheaper but still good option is a Coleman steel-belted cooler. They're half the price and will still hold their chill. In a pinch, any cooler that can be sealed that has frozen water bottles in it should do the job. You'll just have to be mindful of how much ice you still have.

Ensuring that you package your meat in the best possible way preserves the meat's natural flavor, color, and taste. Using the wrong containers would mean that the meat would have an altered taste, which could also be unhealthy. To avoid odors and changes in the taste of your meat, it is best to use a healthier packaging option. You can find some of these in regular stores and even on some online hunting stores.

Keep in mind that it's always easier for you to keep your meat clean than clean out the meat later on. So it's so important to be careful. As you prepare your meat, make sure you can drop the temperature of the meat to under 40 F degrees/ 5 C degrees, but prevent it from freezing. Remember that this temperature doesn't kill bacteria—it slows the growth, so it is still susceptible to spoilage if you're not careful.

Before you store your meat, remember that you should rinse off as much of the blood as possible and scrape away any blood that has already coagulated. The pH of blood makes it particularly susceptible to growing bacteria. Get rid of the water used before putting the meat into a game bag to protect it. Remember, game bags are preferred over plastic in most cases because they're breathable, and this allows the meat to chill quicker.

If the air is not cool enough for you to leave your meat out, get a cooler with some ice packs that won't melt into water. This will allow you to chill the meat without worrying about excess moisture. Some coolers can keep their chill for several days sometimes. Choosing a safe storage option is the perfect way to keep your meat fresh for longer.

(Tip: One trick that I love to use is adding citric acid. This mild organic acid can be sprayed right onto your meat to help keep your meat safer. It will slow down the growth of bacteria, which can make the difference between good or lousy meat if you're traveling with it in warm weather.)

TRANSPORTATION

Finally, it's essential to consider how to transport your meat home. One consideration is how you get home—did you drive there? Did you fly somewhere on a hunting trip? Did you travel for several days to get there? Depending upon how far away you are, you'll have different options to bring your harvest home. If you live relatively close to the hunting grounds, simply bagging it up and driving home with the meat in a cooler should be enough. However, if you've got a long trip ahead of you, you'll need to make sure whatever you're using to carry your meat will be durable enough to keep the meat cool, clean, and safe while still fitting any restrictions you may have.

The simplest way to do this is to start by putting everything in sealable bags or containers. Ziploc bags or something similar work well because they will be easily stored flat when they're not in use, and you'll be able to pack them tightly into a cooler if necessary. When using zipper bags of any kind that seal, using ice will be suitable.

Store your meat in a durable cooler for hunting. If you took a styrofoam cooler out into the field with you because it was lighter, it probably wouldn't be durable enough for you to travel with. This is especially the case if you fly home from your hunting trip. When you fly home, you want to be sure that your cooler won't leak. If you're flying, use the cooler as a carry-on and check it between flights to make sure you don't need to replace the ice.

When you get home, make sure it gets moved straight into a fridge or freezer, depending upon how you want to store the meat. Keep in mind that it may last just 3-5 days before it needs to get used or frozen when you store your meat. When frozen, it can last another 1-2 years, depending upon how you've taken to freezing it.

(Tip: Freezing in vacuum-sealed packages will keep it the freshest for the longest.)

3

THE ESSENTIAL GUIDE
TO SMALL GAME

Before you get out there and get active, you must understand the ins and outs of the animals you may be encountering. Whether you choose to hunt, knowing more about that animal, what they're likely to do, and how you can leave with a successful bounty will help you immensely. As you read through this chapter, you're getting an essential guide to several common animals.

The first bit of information you're going to get is the habitat for each animal. We'll go over where you're likely to find these animals, as well as when they're likely to be more active. It's easier to hunt certain animals at specific times of the year. By knowing where to look for animals, you dramatically boost your chance of success.

Next, you'll be introduced to key techniques that will help you track the game you're trying to find. By knowing how to track the animals that you'd like to hunt, you'll be more likely to find them as well.

Third, you'll receive some key tips to hunt each of the listed animals successfully. These tips should help you boost your chances of getting your hands on something good. Just being able to spot an animal isn't the only thing that counts— you also have to catch and kill it in a way that doesn't render the meat inedible, and that also isn't inhumane. You've got to balance honoring the life of the kill with being able to keep the meat edible. Some of these animals, such as snapping turtles and bullfrogs, are incredibly difficult to kill, while other animals are so small that it's challenging to shoot them without ruining the flesh. Hopefully, armed with the correct weapon and all the information that you'll need, you'll find that this process is made significantly easier.

≡ A FIELD GUIDE TO SQUIRRELS

When it's time to hunt squirrels, there are four types that you're likely to find, depending on where you live. These are fox squirrels, gray squirrels, Abert's squirrels, and pine squirrels. They each look distinctive in their ways.

Fox squirrels are larger than other species. Their fur is mostly grey, but they've got a rusty orange color to their tails and underbellies. They live in smaller woods that have open areas. They're most commonly found in the eastern part of the United States.

Gray squirrels are the most common ones throughout the region, and eastern gray squirrels are commonly actually black, brown, grey, or white, while western grays are found along the west coast.

Abert's squirrels have long grey-black tufts on their ears and darker fur with white underbellies. They don't store food instead of eating pine needles, cones, and bark during the winter. They can be found in western and southwestern portions of the United States.

Pine squirrels are found on the west coast and are small reddish squirrels. These are the most vocal, so if they catch you hunting, they're likely to warn all the other squirrels in the area as well.

HABITAT

Squirrels are found predominantly in trees, which they use both as a source of shelter and to get their food. Squirrels mostly eat nuts, with the preferred nuts varying from location to location. These intelligent animals know that hiding in the trees is one of the best ways they can avoid being eaten by predators, and they'll do what they can to avoid being out in the open if they sense that danger is near. This means that when you want to hunt them, you're going to have a hard time finding them.

The trees make for the perfect shelter for them since most predators can't get through the branches. Foxes, coyotes, and other animals on the ground can't get them as soon as they climb into a tree. While some felines can get at them in the trees, they can run to the tips of the branches they're on, which won't support the weight of most of them. And, when hawks or falcons go after them, they can dart through the branches much better than the birds can navigate through them while flying.

Of course, this means that you're going to be hard-pressed to get a squirrel as soon as it gets into the branches. If you want to track and kill your squirrel successfully, you'll need to draw them out into the open without them detecting your presence.

TRACKING

Tracking a squirrel isn't as hard as you might think, but it requires a lot of patience. Be willing to sit around and wait for something to appear. If you know that squirrels present from other signs, such as seeing chewed-up branches, the husks of nuts, or you can hear them nearby, you know that you're in the right spot. From there, it's all about waiting it out until one wanders in your path.

No squirrel will wander in front of you if you're out making a racket around you. Be quiet about it if you want to coax them to feel comfortable enough to appear in your area. To look for signs of a squirrel, consider these points:

- Squirrel nests: These look like balls of leaves with a few twigs poking out. They enter inside from the side, along the branch. If you can spot these nests, there's a good chance of squirrels in the general area.
- Shredded nuts on the ground: After a squirrel digs up acorns, they prefer to eat them right there. They'll tear the acorn shells up into smaller pieces, which you'll find all over the ground.
- Bark biting: Squirrels will chew along the most common routes they take as they go up and down trees. This leaves a scent mark on them, especially as they rub their cheeks over them. These will look like long, chewed-up strips of bark.

TIPS FOR SUCCESSFUL HUNTING

When you choose to hunt squirrels, the first thing to keep in mind is that they are rarely active when the weather is terrible. Squirrels are the most active in the first hours of daybreak and the later afternoon. This means that the best time to head out would be the first hours of the morning, especially if it's sunny. They avoid being out in bad weather, just like you probably want to do as well. If you're going to have better luck catching squirrels, consider these tips.

Still Hunting

When you still hunt, you sit quietly and wait for the squirrels to come to your area. Hiding somewhere that serves as a natural hiding spot should encourage squirrels to slowly move around more than they feel comfortable that there are no threats around. These animals will often alert their friends in the trees, so you want to be out of sight as much as possible.

Once you've identified a squirrel, you can slowly and carefully stalk them from tree to tree. This involves carefully moving from one area to the next, moving slowly and quietly while listening and scanning the area. You also must make sure the background is safe to shoot before getting ready to do so.

Throw Rocks

Sometimes, you can fool squirrels into thinking that there's another predator somewhere else if you throw rocks against trees. This may make a squirrel appear as it bolts from one area to find somewhere else safe. However, they don't give you a very long window of opportunity before they're off. You'll need to be ready to make a quick shot. Squirrel calls You can mimic the sounds squirrels make with a few common tactics. You could always buy a squirrel call that will do it for you, or you can use your gun and some coins. A coin against the butt plate may imitate the barking sound squirrels make, while two coins together can mimic feeding chatter. This could entice some reluctant squirrels to make their presence known.

Leaf Sounds

When squirrels sense predators, they remain still and out of sight. If you want to encourage a squirrel to approach, one of the easiest ways to do so is to make it sound like squirrels are active in the area again. By stirring at leaves around you, making quick rustling sounds in the leaves in a broken pattern, you mimic the sound of a digging squirrel looking for food. This should mean that it is safe for other squirrels to approach.

Hunt with a Partner

Squirrels are brilliant. They are well-known for running a circle around a tree, constantly staying out of your sights by keeping the tree between you and them. However, if you have a second person there to hunt with you, you can have one person sitting out of sight while the other person makes the squirrel move. The hunter can then shoot.

A FIELD GUIDE TO RABBITS

Rabbits are quick. However, their meat is almost unparalleled in taste. If you want to hunt rabbits, you'll need to know where to spot them. Thankfully, they're relatively easy to find because they prefer places where they can take care of all their needs in one go. They want to know that they can get food, water, and shelter within a relatively small area.

HABITAT

Typically, rabbits will eat as close to their cover as possible, nibbling on grass, shoots, or flowers. They'll also happily enjoy grain from fields or bark from trees. They rarely require too much water, so waiting next to a water source isn't the most effective answer. They're able to keep water from their foods easily, so they'll avoid water if they think it's dangerous.

Typically, you want to hunt in areas with thick cover if you want a rabbit. They'll hide in briars or in areas where the native grass grows thick. The grass provides a source of food and a place where they can hide. They will hide underground as well, taking up unused burrows from digging animals. They'll live their entire lives in a relatively small range of space, usually a few acres at a time, so you'll need to keep this in mind before hunting. If you can find signs of a rabbit nearby, you know it's somewhere close.

TRACKING

Being able to track rabbits will help you immensely when hunting. From being able to spot their footprints to signs of scat or that they've been eating lately, you will do much better on your hunt if you can spot where they are.

Signs of scat

Rabbit scat is a simple way to find out whether there are rabbits nearby as well. They are tiny pellets, between quarter inch to half inch in diameter. It's round and somewhat wrinkly or fibrous. If there is snow on the ground, it may also be marked with orange or reddish urine. They usually leave behind just a few pellets at a time unless they've been there for a while.

Signs of rabbit snacks

When you identify rabbit scat in a pile, you'll also probably find signs of feeding. Typically, the signs of feeding are little snippets in the stems and wood. You'll notice a clean 45-degree cut when twigs are less than . inch in diameter.

Bark gnawing

Rabbits will gnaw at wood if they don't have any other opportunity to get the food they need. If you notice the other signs and nibbles on bark near levels that the rabbits can reach, there's probably a rabbit nearby.

TIPS FOR SUCCESSFUL HUNTING

To hunt successfully, you'll need first to track down signs that there are rabbits nearby. Then, be able to get started. To make it easier, consider these different actions as well.

Rabbit dogs

Rabbit dogs are incredibly beneficial. Those who know how to hunt and are trained well can lead the rabbit right back to where you're ready to hunt it. However, you will need to make sure that the dog is trained for the task. Even then, your dog may go after the rabbit as soon as you shoot it, ruining it to retrieve the flesh.

Walk or stalk

When you hunt on your own, you may need to walk through the cover to make the rabbit run or stalk it somewhere near a rabbit's habitat. Walking works well in a group, primarily if you can communicate when you've flushed a rabbit out, and it's heading toward someone else. Stalking is best alone, especially in the winter, where you can track steps. Keep in mind that by the time you spot a rabbit, it's probably already been watching you. You'll need to be careful not to spook it.

Hunt along edges

Natural edges take advantage of rabbits' habitat, such as the line between a forest and a field or heavy cover and somewhere less populated. Hunting along the edges means you're more likely to spot a rabbit.

≡ A FIELD GUIDE TO GROUSE AND PARTRIDGES

HABITAT

Grouse and partridges eat both plants and insects, with acorns being a staple in the winter months to increase body fat for spring reproduction. They may enjoy berries, shoots, and other nuts as well when they can find them. They are not very picky! While they require water like all other animals, they can usually get enough food or drink from morning dew. They only seek standing or running water out readily when it's been dry, or they'll also enjoy it if they stumble upon it along with their foraging.

Typically, it's more important for you to consider the shelter of the grouse/partridge when trying to find them. They love to live in wooded areas—in particular, they love forests. They rarely hide in the trees unless they're threatened, but they enjoy the woody cover.

They will usually stay within a mile of where they were hatched, meaning that it's relatively easy to find them. The male's drum in the spring attracts females and has even smaller ranges than females, who will follow the drumming male and hunt down their nesting site.

For the best of luck, go hunting on sunny days in the fall, when there's just a little wind. You may hear them walking around during this time. They're most active late and early in the day, but you may find them. However, when it's windy, they'll stay hidden in trees.

TRACKING

If you're interested in finding grouse/partridge, one of the best ways to do so is to locate areas where there are acorns all over the ground. This is especially the case in the fall if you want to find birds enjoying them.

As you walk around, consider pausing if you think that a grouse/partridge might be present. They sit still as long as you're walking by them at a steady pace. However, if you stop moving, they may think they've been found, and instead of remaining in place, they'll run. This means that you'll have the opportunity to get them.

(Tip: The easiest way to track them is to walk or drive down gravel dirt roads. The grouse/partridge eats little rocks for their digestive system. They tend to stand still if they are spooked, so catching them off guard on the road gives you a wide-open shot.)

TIPS FOR SUCCESSFUL HUNTING

Grouse/Partridge hunting isn't always easy. You're looking for a small bird that can easily hide or fly away, and you're in it's habitat. It can be even harder to locate your kill after shooting one, especially if you have no clue where it may have gone. Consider these important tips if you want to hunt grouse/partridge effectively. Start scouting the area in spring Since these birds don't stray far from where they hatched, you'll know where they'll be in fall by looking in the spring for the birds. You'll be able to listen for the drumming males in the spring to get a general idea of where they're likely to populate. You may even hear chicks chirping to tell you where they have been nesting. By finding these locations, you'll be likely to find grouse ready for hunting in the fall as well.

Finding Prime Habitat

Grouse/Partridge prefers to nest in areas where a forest has begun a secondary succession. This means that the area has had some significant disturbance, such as a fire or natural storm that decimated the original plants. Then, 5 to 12 years after that point, there is new growth thriving in the secondary succession. This is prime land for grouse, and you're likely to find them.

Second Flushes

When a bird flies uphill to avoid you, it won't go as far as a bird that is flying downhill. Usually, it's easier to hunt those going uphill than those going downhill.

A FIELD GUIDE TO DOVES

Doves, especially mourning doves, are a tasty choice if you want to hunt them. Most hunters are likely to focus on where they feed, and for a good reason. If you're going to find your doves to catch, the best thing you can do is know where you should be looking. These birds can pose a bit of a challenge as they move quickly through the air. However, if you know what you're doing, they can be caught.

HABITAT

Doves eat seeds primarily, which means that looking in areas where weeds and grass grow and produce seeds is a great way to hunt them down. They have feet designed for perching, so you'll want to look for areas where they can perch to get their food.

They'll also go out of the way to get water at least twice per day. This is easy during wet seasons, but they're likely to visit ponds and streams during dryer seasons. In particular, they need somewhere they can get water, and if you find areas where they can get water without cover, you may catch them drinking. Doves migrate, flying north in the summer and south in the fall and winter, so plan your season accordingly.

TRACKING

Before you get started with hunting, you'll need to know how to track them. Typically, the best thing you can do is choose a location to hunt and stick to it. If you've chosen a suitable location, the birds should come. Keep these tips in mind to ensure you're tracking well.

Scouting layouts

Scouting the layout is about spending a few days viewing the field before you decide to hunt it. You want to know what you're working with. You want to know what's going on with the area before you choose to hunt there. Get to know what a day or two of activity looks like before jumping into the action. Sometimes, seeing what happens at dawn will show you what you can expect to see the next day. Watch the birds early on to notice their habits. You'll also get the ability to understand the flight paths they take. The flight paths that they take are usually the paths they leave as well.

High ground

Look for the high ground before you get started. The high spots are the most likely to attract doves. It becomes a natural flight target. If you can stand between a hill and somewhere woody, you've got an excellent chance to see some doves flying over.

Near water

Setting up by the water in the afternoon is a great way to catch doves who need to get some drinks before heading off to roost for the night. They want places that are low with little brush so they can land and see their surroundings.

TIPS FOR SUCCESSFUL HUNTING

To up your chances of catching doves, there are a few steps that will help you. Shoot high birds Shooting high means shooting overhead birds and within your range. However, this is also one of the most challenging shots to make if you don't know what you're doing.

Use a retriever

Because hunting should not produce waste, it might be easier to have a retriever to help if you're hunting in a heavily planted field. A good retriever will be able to help you find birds quicker and easier.

Look for activity

Every so often throughout the afternoon, there will be periods where the doves fly about more often. They will fly for 5 or 10 minutes, then be relatively inactive. Keeping track of this and being ready to land your shots will help.

Follow through with the swing

When you shoot doves, one of the most common mistakes is cutting the swing of the shot short. As you track your target, you're swinging to keep your gun aiming at it. If you don't continue the swing after pulling the trigger, you're going to miss the shot.

A FIELD GUIDE TO QUAILS AND PHEASANTS

Hunting quail/Pheasants can be highly exciting as you make your way through hunting. These birds depend highly on the weather because they can't store enough energy for extended cold periods. This means that they must go out into the snow to hunt as much as they can. This is especially important to consider because they can't dig easily through the snow. When you can find them, however, you get a huge benefit: They taste amazing.

HABITAT

Quail/Pheasants are edge species—they prefer to live in areas with dense covers within walking distance for food. They primarily enjoy waste grain in fields or weed seeds. If you can find somewhere with these criteria, you're likely to find quail/pheasant around as well. The best area to find them is within about 25 yards of the edge between a weedy field and a culti-vated grain field.

Typically, they get enough water from morning dew and rarely seek out watering holes unless it's been exceptionally dry lately. They're left too vulnerable to water holes and try to avoid being out in the open.

Once you locate a covey of quails/pheasants, you're likely to continue to find them in the same area each year. They'll come to the exact location if they consistently get the resources they need to survive.

TRACKING

When you want to track quail/pheasant, there are a few places you can look that are usually likely to provide what you're looking for. However, lately, there has been a decline in wild quail/pheasant as they lose their habitat, so you may find it harder to locate them. Typically, they are found somewhere that is both open and woody. They like briars and other areas that will keep them covered.

Keep in mind the following:

- Quail/Pheasants like to enjoy seeds in the fields in the morning.
- They like to rest midday under some cover.
- They like a snack in the afternoon on the weedy field.
- They sleep in grassy, weedy areas at night.

TIPS FOR SUCCESSFUL HUNTING

The hunting process for quail and pheasants can be tedious as you go through looking for them. However, you can make it easier for yourself by remembering and implementing tips such as the following:

Get a hunting dog

A good hunting dog is highly effective for flushing out quail. Make sure that your dog is well-trained, so they don't rush and scare birds. Training a dog to use a slow approach to get close will help to flush them out.

Practice Marksmanship

One of the most critical skills you'll need is to train yourself to shoot to kill. Quail and pheasants are quick and skilled at flying. If you can't shoot quickly in a wave of confusion, you're going to miss the kill. To help with this, try practicing shooting with a friend, having them throw several targets in a quick rush while you try to shoot them down.

Know the Habits

Quail and pheasants are very predictable. They'll repeatedly come to the same fields, will rest, and eat at the same time. By learning the routines of the quail you're hunting, be able to eliminate a lot of the confusion of where they are at any point in time.

Look for the Covey Rise

When you flush out a covey of quail/pheasant, and they all rush up, you may feel quite excited about it. You're probably going to be thrilled to see them all at once. However, keep in mind that you should focus on one bird at a time. Usually, you can take one or two at a time within a few seconds as you get better at hunting.

A FIELD GUIDE TO DUCKS

Hunting ducks is a bit of a difficult pastime if you don't know what you're doing, but it can be deliciously fulfilling. Traditionally, hunters hide in a blind either over water or in a field, while hunters display decoys to make it look like other ducks are already there.

The purpose of this is to lure other birds to the area. If they see other ducks and geese hanging out in the area, they will assume it's a safe place to rest and enjoy some food, so they'll take some time to land there as well.

The best way to know how to get started with ducks is to make sure that you scout areas before. Make sure you choose locations that birds have already traditionally visited to ensure that you make it convincing.

HABITAT

As waterfowl, ducks will be found near water. They need this for roosting and loafing. They will need to return to the water at some point, so if you can find the water, you're likely also to find them. If you've seen them hiding in these areas on their own already, you're likely to hunt them in the coming days.

Look for areas with shallow wetlands filled with seed-producing plants, especially in the early season. They'll enjoy being able to munch on the plants that they can find. Rivers, marshes, creeks, open water, or even flooded fields, such as rice or soybeans, are quick to attract ducks because of the water and food. Make sure that you check the policies for hunting, and you check whether you can legally hunt in the area where you're scoping out ducks. You may try to hunt on developed land.

Typically, most people will come in to hunt on an opening day for the season. You're likely to find that you've got plenty of newly hatched birds making their first migration, and they'll be much easier to trick than others who have had a few rodeos and know what to look out for.

You want to pay attention to the weather when hunting as well. When there's a strong north wind, or when the weather is colder, you'll find that birds are flying south, looking for warmth. If you're hunting, sunshine and wind will be perfect. This is especially the case for mallards, who may also choose to stick it out as the weather cools.

Sometimes, you may even find that ducks will return north during the season. When there is a freeze that pushes them south, followed by a quick thaw, they will often return to the area they just left, at which point they're less wary than they were before as well. You may also find that at the very end of the season, as birds move north to their breeding grounds, you might catch some. They are so caught up trying to get back for a mating that they forget to pay attention to prevent themselves from being hunted.

TRACKING

You ultimately have five different options for hunting and tracking ducks. If you're somewhere where ducks remain, you're likely to find them in the water. You can choose to hunt them through these options:

1. Decoys: With this method, you set out decoys all over a field or in the water and then hide in a blind to wait for the birds to come around. Then, when they land, you can hunt.

2. Pass shooting: This involves shooting at flight lines as they pass in your shotgun range. You essentially figure out how the birds are flying, stay in the line, and wait for them to come by. You then shoot as they pass over you.

3. Jump shooting: With jump shooting, you sneak up on ducks on the water, then fire as they take flight. This is typically done near shorelines.

4. Float hunts: This involves floating on a river in either a canoe or a kayak and shooting at unsuspecting birds. You'll have to depend on the river during this time, which can be difficult as well.

5. Skull boat shoots: This form of hunting involves using a skiff and paddle to get within the shooting range of ducks. Then, you'll have to shoot quickly. This is perhaps the hardest of the methods.

TIPS FOR SUCCESSFUL HUNTING

If you want to hunt ducks, you need to keep in mind that they can be a bit difficult. Most birds can be tricky to hunt, but this is especially the case with smaller ones. This means that you need to be prepared with a vast arsenal to help you with the process.

Don't forget the camo

Camo is essential to keeping yourself hidden. However, if you're going to be hunting on a kayak or some other boat, you want to keep your boat concealed as well. You can do this with a camo cord. Essentially, you just put some cord across your kayak that's been spaced roughly a foot apart and then weave in a bunch of natural vegetation found in the area. This will help you conceal the boat from sight and may even remain in place all season long if you're careful. You'll have an easier time sneaking up on everything in this manner.

Hunt later

Typically, ducks will migrate with cold fronts so they can use the strong tailwinds. If you have a cold front coming through your area, make sure you don't leave early. Stay later into the morning so you can be there when flocks may stop to take a rest before getting on their way.

Know when to remove the decoys

While decoys can be a great tool for you, they can also put you at a serious disadvantage if you don't know what you're doing. Many ducks may be afraid of them, especially later in the season when they realize that all the stationary ducks they've seen seem to show that there will be shots fired. If the decoys remain in place, they're likely to have problems. Late in the season, pull them in and use calls instead.

Be patient

This should be a rule for all the games you're hunting. Patience is a virtue. It's a huge mistake if you accidentally flush out all the ducks from the roost before dawn has even hit. If you wait for first light and the ducks to spread out on their own before creeping out to set up shop, you're less likely to startle away the ducks, and you'll likely have the ducks return later on to rest, meaning that overall, you'll have more shooting opportunities.

Check the winds

Pay attention to the wind so you can position the decoys and blinds. If you can't tell which way the wind is blowing, you can try squeezing a bit of talcum powder or fine soil in the air and see which way it goes. That's the direction the wind is blowing.

Camouflage the gun

While you might hide with white gloves and jackets, you still need to hide your shotgun. These are highly visible in the snow, especially if you're also wearing all white. You want to consider covering up your barrel with white medical gauze to hide it while hunting in snowy conditions.

A FIELD GUIDE TO TURKEYS

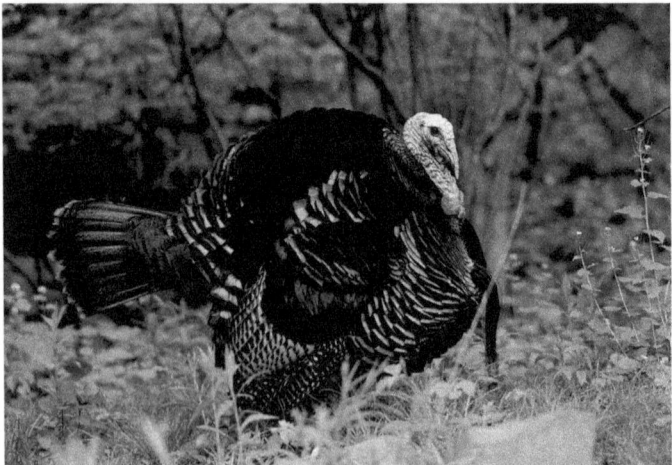

Turkeys eat a wide range of things out in the wild, starting on bugs and quickly moving to acorns and fresh greens. The fatty nuts they eat prepare them to survive for the winter while also providing them with a delicious taste. They can usually be spotted in the early morning, hunting for grasshoppers or sipping at the water. If you want to track them down, you'll need first to know where to look.

HABITAT

Typically, you'll find turkeys hunting for food or water. On spring days, they may not need to visit water sources if it's rained recently - they can enjoy standing in water puddles or on leaves. Tracking water sources is a great way to spot where these birds are at any point in time.

Turkeys will usually stick to a relatively small range—typically only 2000 acres. Toms will spend their time in even more limited ranges because the females come to the males while the females roam. The entire flock is likely to stick to the same range unless disturbed, and when they leave, there's a good chance that more birds will enter the area.

TRACKING

The best thing that you can do when tracking turkeys is to start with scouting. Start by looking for signs of dropped feathers, scratches, and strut marks on the grounds, or even droppings. Tracks are commonly found as well, especially near water sources.

It's usually a good idea to scout the week before you're ready to hunt. This will help you spot out the various areas where the turkeys prefer to stay. You should also make it a point to track early in the morning. If you get lucky, you'll find a male strutting and attracting females. As he courts his hens, he's more or less setting up his own space. He's going to stay in that area unless you disturb him. If you wait for him in the morning, you're likely to find him around in the afternoon in a similar area. Setting up where he was in the morning is the best way to find him in the afternoon. And, if you watch his routine over a few days, you're more likely to find them. They will stick to the same routine as much as they can, making them easy to predict.

TIPS FOR SUCCESSFUL HUNTING

When you're out hunting, there are several things that you can do to help boost your chances of success. Remember these tips if you want to have a good chance at catching your turkey. Turkeys have a grand vision, so they're likely to see you if you're moving too much.

Camouflage matters

The best thing that you can do when you're hunting turkey ensures that you can camouflage yourself. Make sure that you're hiding somewhere that they can't see you, and use camouflage on your tools. Turkeys will know what to look out for—they'll see your skin or hair as a sign to run. They may even notice a flash of teeth. Their vision is exceptional, and you need to hide well.

Stillness

Just camouflage isn't enough either. You need to remain as still as possible. They're likely to catch you if you're moving around too much as the camouflage will move with it. They've got great vision, and if you're not careful to be still and silent, the turkey is likely to leave quickly before you spot it.

Use a blind or large tree

A blind can be your best tool when hunting turkeys. If you can't use a blind, you'll need a tree that's big enough that your silhouette will be hidden, and you'll be able to sit in the shadows as much as possible. However, in a blind, you'll be able to move around a bit more, and you'll be able to enjoy coffee or something else inside of it, as turkeys can't smell.

Don't stalk it

Stalking turkeys is rarely a good idea. Turkeys are much more likely to spot your movements if you're trying to stalk them when they're out of range and you try to approach them. Instead, you can remember what they're doing and where they're doing it so you can focus on them in the future. You're likely to find them better if you do.

≡ A FIELD GUIDE TO GEESE

Canada geese are well known for their wide range of migrations. They fly south in wide V formations that are quick to catch the eye of all who see them. However, for hunters, this marks the beginning of a very important time: Hunting season.

Canada goose hunting has become very specialized lately, with people creating calling tools and more just to get the kill. They have learned the ins and outs of being able to lure geese in to use for their own, and you can learn some serious tips to do the same as well.

HABITAT

Geese will be found in primarily the same habitat as ducks and other waterfowl. You can expect them to be enjoying time in wet places, from rivers to lakes and more. They don't care where the water source is, and they just want to have somewhere they can hide and meet their needs.

Geese will display where they're at, however, announcing their presence with their cries. They will usually travel in large flocks, in huge V-shaped wedges. They'll break up here and there, but if you call the geese as you see and hear them, you may attract them to you.

They travel south for the winter and then north again in the warmer summers, riding on the tails of cold fronts, so pay close attention to the weather. They're a bit more likely to hunker down in cold weather than ducks are, and they aren't about digging out their holes in the snow to eat.

TRACKING

Rather than tracking geese, it's more about waiting for them to arrive. Like with ducks, one of the best ways to lure them in is to set up a blind so they can't locate you and then set up decoys, remembering that as the season goes on, they're likely to be hesitant to approach them if they don't know the source. You'll likely want to study their habits before hunting, and remember that you are better off waiting to settle in after they've already taken off for their morning feeding.

You might enjoy setting up an elaborate blind, but keep in mind that after a few shots, you're likely to spook the birds to move elsewhere, at which point, you can either find another body of water, or you can wait for more to fly in.

Remember that while tracking these birds, you must be as motionless as possible and only shoot when they've approached you enough that you know you can catch them. Keep in mind that if you notice they seem wary, they're probably spotting something that makes them nervous. You might need to change up your layout if you want to attract them to your area. They may look reluctant about landing, or they might even take off at the last minute instead of landing within your range. These geese are growing increasingly wary, which means it will be challenging to catch them.

TIPS FOR SUCCESSFUL HUNTING

To hunt geese successfully, several tips can help you immensely with the process. Knowing how to call to set up your decoys, you're likely to attract geese your way. Figure out what works best for you and change your strategy if something isn't working for you any longer.

The Call

Goose calls can be beneficial to entice birds to land within your range. You can get them in three different styles: Resonant chambers, flutes, and short - reeds. Typically, resonant chambers are the easiest to use, but they're also very limited. You can't make as many sounds. Flute calls are harder to use but make more sounds, but they're also usually mellower.

Short - reed

calls will have the widest range of sounds and are louder, with less air needed than the other options. The short-reed call is the favored variety among hunters and will be your best bet if you're serious about hunting geese.

Setting up Decoys

Decoys will be vital, and you'll want to set them up in areas with brilliant cover for you. Your job is to remain covered, and if you can hunt where you can hide, you're going to see significant improvements in your ability to hunt. Find rows of grass that might have a dip in terrain where you'd be able to hide as well. Avoid getting yourself stuck in the same place for too long, however, or the geese will get to know where you are.

Don't choose several different decoys

If you're not wise with the decoys you set up, then you can run into trouble. This is especially true if you mix them up and create a mismatched look that sets the geese off that there's something wrong. Stick to just one kind of decoy for the best results.

Stay out of the way

While it might be convenient to place yourself in line with the bird's approach, you're also going to scare them off when they recognize the signs that hunters are present. Instead of being where the geese are, place yourself ten yards to the side of where they'll be landing or parallel with the wind. This will help you stay hidden, and you're more likely to land the shot.

☰ A FIELD GUIDE TO BULLFROGS

North American bullfrogs are the largest frogs that you can locate in North America, and vary from greens to browns, and are usually somewhat blotchy. They also taste great when you fry frog legs. These frogs have been appearing and spreading throughout North America, out-competing other native frog species, and are invasive in many areas. They're quite large and are starving, so they'll continue to seek out new waters and expand their range, little by little. They were initially introduced in the early 1900s as a food source and expanded their territory.

Hunting these animals can be tricky, as they're tough to kill effectively, but hunting them can yield plenty of food for you to enjoy. Their meat tastes like a cross between fish and chicken and can be an enjoyable addition to your diet. There's a good chance that you're likely to find them with a bit of perseverance, and you can catch them with a net, a fishing rod, or even your hands if you wanted to.

They're willing to eat just about anything they can get their tongues on, including fish, mice, or even snakes. They're not afraid of much, but they will run away from you if you try to catch them.

Keep in mind that you need to know what the laws are for hunting bullfrogs in your area. Some places may require you to kill them before you transport them.

HABITAT

Bullfrogs will live anywhere they can find food. They're invasive on the western side of the continent, and they're easy to find just about anywhere you'd find other frogs. Look for them in ponds and lakes, and you're bound to find them lurking beneath the water's surface.

Many people hunt for them at night, choosing to shine flashlights and look for the reflections of their eyes.

To find them, look in ponds and marshes. Listen in the evening before going out to hunt—you'll hear their calls and will know that you're in the right spot. They'll usually all croak together. It's a loud, deep croak.

TRACKING

Tracking bullfrogs is as simple as listening for their tell-tale cry. You'll hear the tell-tale guttural noises they make, and you're also likely to see them around. If you're hunting at night, you'll be able to see the reflections of their eyes in the water. However, if you're somewhere where frogs can be heard, and you're in bullfrog territory, there are probably bullfrogs present as well.

TIPS FOR SUCCESSFUL HUNTING

Hunting bullfrogs can be tricky if you don't know what you're doing, especially if you go into it bare-handed. They are quick to spook, and they'll often dart right out of your reach if you're not careful. However, if you're armed with a fishing pole, you're likely to catch them. By using a hook just right, you can fish them up quickly. Alternatively, you can chase them down and use your hands, a bucket, a net, or anything else. Even pronged grabbers you can use to snap them up to pull them in if you wanted to. You could even shoot one if you had a gun and were close enough, but this isn't the most recommended way to do so.

Hooking a bobber

One of the more efficient ways to catch a bullfrog is to put a hook directly on top and on the bottom of a bobber, with some sort of lure to catch them. You can add a bit of bait or grasshopper onto one end of the hook. Then, wait for the frog to latch onto it and reel them in.

Hunt at nighttime

It's easier to see bullfrogs at night. They're more likely to come out on land when it's no longer sunny enough to dry them out almost immediately after they go out. To monitor them, you can use an LED flashlight to search for them slowly. Bigger bullfrogs will have wide-set eyes that are further apart than most other eyes you see.

Use a canoe if possible

Your footprints are likely to startle away any bullfrogs you're hunting down, even if you try your hardest to be quiet as you go. It's better to make it a point to slowly creep up on a canoe in the water, moving gently than to walk along the shore. But, if you are hunting on land, just try to move as quietly as you can.

Jacking bullfrogs

By shining a bright light into the bullfrog within about 10 yards, you can "jack" the bullfrog. You essentially put the frog in a trance, similar to how deer pause at headlights. This allows you to rush toward it and catch it with your bare hands or with anything else that you have.

Remember to be firm, but not too firm

Don't grab a bullfrog too roughly. We're not out trying to hurt them, and just because we're hunting them doesn't mean that we need to forget about their comfort and well-being. Don't cause unnecessary pain by squeezing them. Hold them with the same pressure you'd use on a bar of soap, and hold them grasping around upper thighs and legs held together so they can't jump away.

Kill it quickly

If you're trying to kill the bullfrog, you can either bash their head or cut off their head. They are known for making you think they're dead, only to try to rush away mid-skinning suddenly. You want to desensitize it and then kill it. A few swift blows to the head should do it. Make sure it's fully dead before you skin it. Some people prefer removing the head before field dressing to make sure the frog is dead.

☰ A FIELD GUIDE TO SNAPPING TURTLES

If you live somewhere filled with snapping turtles, the first thing that you need to do is confirm that you may hunt them where you live or where you are going. You may choose to use traps, or you might simply snatch one up if the opportunity arises. Either way, hunting for a turtle can provide you with a delicious meal. One of the easiest ways to get your hands on a snapping turtle is to create a trap for them and set it out somewhere that will help you catch it.

Keep in mind that snapping turtles are dangerous: If you put your hand in harm's way, they can bite your finger right off. They're also quick and can flip themselves over, so even if you think that you've flipped one over and it'll be okay to grab, think again. Their claws are also quite dangerous. However, when you grab them by their tails and hold them out of reach of your body, they can't do anything at all.

Spotting a snapping turtle as opposed to other turtles that may be less dangerous is pretty straightforward. They usually have duller shells that may even be covered in moss or algae. Its tail and head won't retract fully either. And you'll notice that they have sharp claws on yellow feet, plus a massive, thick neck. They can also move quickly on land.

HABITAT

Snapping turtles can be found in a wide range of North America, from Southern Alberta to Central Texas in the US. They live only in either fresh or brackish water but prefer water muddy and loaded with plant life. This allows them to hide easier, meaning they can snag their prey easier than well. They will usually spend their time in the water but will make their way onto land when it's time to lay eggs.

They can be found in many types of water and aren't that picky, so long as it isn't saltwater. They can be found in lakes, ponds, streams, rivers, or even marshes and swamps. They're solitary creatures that rarely have many social interactions beyond mating.

Keep in mind that they may even bury themselves in mud, leaving only their eyes and nostrils exposed. They may even leave out their tongues, which they wiggle around in the water to attract fish to eat.

TRACKING

Typically, you don't track turtles. You either find them or you don't. It's usually to set up a snapping turtle trap, which you can use to help yourself find them. Follow these steps for a simple turtle trap that will help you catch some in no time.

1. Start with a long strip of chicken wire. It should be large enough to create a wire trap roughly 2 feet in diameter. Then, using tie wire, tie each of the holes as you work your way up, essentially stitching the chicken wire. Do so up four feet.

2. Cut the wire above the last two feet. You'll have a strip of wire that's 6 feet x 2 feet.

3. Take the flat piece of wire to the top of your 4' tube, attach it all the way around with tie wire, and then cut off the excess. This closes off the trap. Put the closed end down with the open end facing up.

4. Take a dip net and cut off 7-8 inches, having an open end on each side.

5. Put the narrow end of the dip net inside the cage. Then, tie the rest of it to the top of the trap. Use strong nylon to do this, weaving it in place.

6. Cut a doorway using a wire cutter to create 10 inches on two sides of the door and 16 inches on the last side. This can be opened and closed to let you reach into the trap.

7. Use a foot of nylon string to tie to the narrow end of the dip net on each side of the trap to create a funnel.

8. Tie some bait a foot away from the narrow end of the dip net and make sure the turtle can't get it without entering the trap.

TIPS FOR SUCCESSFUL HUNTING

Set the trap somewhere it's not going to drown the turtle When you are hunting, you don't want to drown the turtle before you get out unintentionally. You'll like the trap to be designed so the turtle can't somehow dislodge it and make it fall into the water. If the turtle drowns, it probably won't still be fresh by the time you get it.

Choose good bait

The bait wins over snapping turtles. Make it a point to choose out bait like chicken or fish that it can smell, but it won't reach unless it gets into the trap. This should help you ensure you get your catch.

Stun before killing

Snapping turtles are dangerous. You're going to want to stun it before you reach inside of it. The best way to do this is to smash it in the head, pushing it inward toward the shell.

4

STEP-BY-STEP HOW TO FIELD DRESS

Man has traditionally had to turn to hunt; it has been part of the human heritage since the beginning of time. If you don't hunt, you don't eat, and if you don't eat, you don't live. Hunting has been a major way of sustenance, not just for food production but also for other resources. Animal fur, for example, can serve as clothing when the weather is too cold to go without it. We may be among the most intelligent species in the world, but we indeed aren't built the best for surviving in a perfect state of nature. With animal skins, we can thrive in temperatures well below what we'd typically be able to tolerate usually.

Before we begin, remember this: Nature is preserved. The world quickly turns into a concrete jungle, and hunters must protect the animals if we want to continue hunting. If we don't protect nature, who will? As a hunter, respect the world around you. You should revere the wilderness that provides you with the sustenance that keeps you going and honor and protect it from harm. Therefore, many states & places like Ontario make hunters go through a course before issuing any hunting licenses.

Following specific guidelines while hunting helps prevent the endangerment of wildlife. The rules we have out there keep everyone safe; they protect you from doing something dangerous and also protect nature from further strain than is sustainable. With the constant urbanization of remove wildlife land, we must protect what is left of it. After all, life is sacred, and even though we as hunters take it, we know we should preserve the species for future hunting. If we go all in and hunt them all to death, there would be nothing left for future hunts. Future generations wouldn't be able to rely on these wonderful natural resources to take care of themselves. As responsible hunters, we must preserve these animals for the future. To preserve the wildlife, many places require you to keep track of how many animals you hunt and to limit what you may target in many situations.

Caring for your kills is just as important as knowing how to hunt responsibly and sustainably. As soon as you get that kill, the clock ticks… You only have so long to field dress the kill before you risk contamination. The wilderness isn't exactly the cleanest place around, and as soon as the immune system stops working, you run into the danger of having the meat grow bacteria. Or, if you don't open the animal up the right way, you could unintentionally contaminate everything with the entrails or brain, both of which are supposed to be kept as far away from the meat as possible. You need to get it cleaned out safely and brought down to a safe temperature as soon as possible to reduce the risk of food-borne illnesses.

Everything about hunting hinges upon your reflexes and speeds. You'll need to respond and catch your prey as quickly as possible. You'll need to field dress quickly, typically in less than an hour, to prevent bacteria from taking hold. To be prepared, you'll need to also have the right equipment on hand for use at a moment's notice.

(Tip: The quicker you field dress your meat and cool, it will dictate how good your meat will taste!)

PREPARING FOR SAFE HUNTING

There are enough risks in hunting to feel you should take on new ones. Make sure that you always take the time to prepare for a safe hunting expedition, ensuring that you're in good physical shape to hunt, you're dressed for hunting, and familiarize yourself with the risks. If you're reading this book, there's a chance you're a complete newbie to hunting, so ensuring that you do nothing too risky will help to protect you in the long run.

PHYSICAL WELLNESS

To protect yourself, avoid hunting if you are not feeling well. This is a recipe for disaster as you could end up contracting a worse sickness. The body is more prone to illness when exposed to conditions that weaken the immune system some more. Take the precaution to keep yourself safe and avoid contracting infections and diseases that could worsen your sickness.

≡ DRESS FOR SUCCESS

When you're out hunting, you expose yourself to many elements that you may need to consider. You might be, for example, out in the weather too cold or wet to get through without winter gear. Or, you could be somewhere that is hot and sunny, in which case you'll still need protection from the sun to prevent sunburn. There's always a risk of animal or insect bites in the forest, and ticks or other blood-sucking animals may be more than happy to take on the free meal if they see some bare skin.

Make sure that you cover your skin with appropriate clothing for the weather. If there are forecasts of rain or snow, make sure you have something waterproof that will help you continue to stay warm. You could also wear several layers, which you can remove or add on as the weather changes throughout the day. Shoes should be appropriate to walk through the terrain you've chosen as well.

(Tip: To be a successful hunter, you need to be prepared for all elements of nature.)

Many hunting areas have regulations about wearing an orange vest for visibility to other people. Make sure that when you're hunting, you follow any regulatory laws. They're there to protect you and while it's a good idea to hide when you're hunting, remember that you don't want someone else to not see you because of your camouflage.

☰ KNOW WARNING SIGNS IN NATURE

Avoid hunting animals that show any symptom of illness. If it's not running as fast as its legs will take it away from you, or it is not as alert as it should be, there is most likely something wrong with the animal. Sick animals could transmit zoonotic diseases to whoever handles or eats them. To prevent illness, make sure that you avoid these animals. If it isn't a challenge for you to hunt, it's probably too good to be true.

You may also want to consider looking out for signs of old, infected illnesses. If there is anything that doesn't look quite right on your kill, there could be a problem, and it's usually better to be safe than sorry. Anything that looks suspicious should be thoroughly examined, and the affected part of the meat should also be cut off to avoid the spread of any infection in the wound.

Suppose it's your first-time field dressing or handling game. In that case, you may not be acquainted with the inner structure of the animal you are hunting, but if you have the slightest sign that something is not right with the game you have hunted, consult someone more experienced than you are or consider disposing of the carcass. Things like blood clots unassociated with the hunting injury, offensive smell, suspicious muscular arrangement, and so on show that something is wrong with the animal.

☰ TIPS FOR FIELD DRESSING SMALL GAME

When you finally get your kill, you're probably eager to ensure that you dress it appropriately. You want to make sure that you treat it well to enjoy the fruits of your labor. Field dress properly means recognizing when and how to make it happen quickly, so the meat is spared. You want to save as much of the meat as possible to avoid wasting the animal, so the sooner you catch onto the necessary actions you'll need to take, the better.

THE PROCESS

The process of field dressing isn't that hard. Especially when you have a smaller game, you rarely need to struggle too much. Your strength is typically enough to cut through skin and bones. Be even more careful—most tools that we use may be too large to use on small squirrels to gut them effectively. If you've never field dressed small game, it's relatively simple. You begin with skinning and gutting (or gutting and skinning in some situations). Then, you simply clean it out, and you're on your way.

Some animals will have a few more steps. Others will have a few less. Luckily for you, we'll be going through all the details, step by step, shortly. Just remember, this isn't necessarily a clean or glamorous process. There will be blood. You may accidentally bust a gut at least once (we've all been there!). You'll find animals that don't look so good once you open them up. Just keep. Not all kills will be that great, and that's okay.

CLEAN IT QUICKLY

One of the most important rules is that you should clean and store your kill as quickly as possible. While some hunters may be fine tying their small game kills to their waists as they continue hunting, the meat will always taste the best when you clean it sooner. This will help you remove any nasty bacteria or other stinky parts sooner rather than later before they foul the meat. The meat can spoil much quicker if the innards are left intact longer. Even if you hunt in colder weather, you still need to clean it quickly. Think of it this way: you are trying to bring down the internal temperature of an animal that has a pelt or feathers designed to insulate it and keep it warm. The temperatures will not drop quickly enough for the meat to be good if you leave it intact, and the digestive enzymes will have the chance to taint the meat.

Most animals can be gutted immediately after you've reclaimed them. Even if you don't want to stop and strip feathers off your bird, you can still remove the guts and let the cooling start. Rabbits and squirrels are easy enough to break down all at once. Just get it over with and be on your way. Your meat will taste the best.

AVOID GUT BUSTING

Gut-busting happens when you nick the digestive system and everything in it comes spilling out. It smells awful and can taint the taste of your meat if you let it. It could even allow for passing food borne bacteria and disease if you're not careful. E. coli and other dangerous pathogens can be found in the guts and can cause problems, which can be made even worse if you cannot keep the meat cool enough.

REMOVE HAIRS

If you are rough or messy with the meat that you're cleaning, you might end up with tiny hairs in the meat after you've skinned them. You could run the meat under running water if you can, or you could burn them off with a lighter, torch, or burner. The best way to avoid the problem is to be more mindful as you skin your meat simply.

POP JOINTS INSTEAD OF CUTTING BONE

Some people like to try cutting right through the bones of their animals. However, this is a dangerous practice. Bones can splinter and leave small, dangerous pieces in the meat that are consumed. Bone shards could also poke straight through vacuum bags if you're not careful. Rather than cutting through bone, make it a point to pop the joint. This will allow you to separate it, breaking nothing, keeping the meat safe from bone shards.

AVOID BRAINS AND ENTRAILS

While field dressing, keep the entrails and brain matter of the animal away from the meat itself. Therefore, from the start, aim for a clean shot. Killing the animal with one shot is more humane and less messy. Shooting the animal around the abdomen could cause a lot of mess during the process of field dressing.

WASHING TOOLS

Wash your tools, but do not wash the animal itself. Suppose you've done everything right while field dressing; you wouldn't have to clean the meat. Washing the dressed game exposes it to contamination. Just place the meat in a bag and store them in an ice-packed cooler to preserve it.

Ensure you wash your hands thoroughly with water and soap, especially if you touch the animal's innards. Your hands are your most valuable tools, after all!. Wash the tools you used, wash the surface you worked on. Everything must be washed with soap and water and properly disinfected. Add bleach to the water you use for washing up afterward. The bleach serves as a disinfectant on the go. Just be mindful never to drink water that has had bleach added to it.

FIELD DRESSING SMALL GAME

Once you've got your kill secured, you will need to process it quickly to keep it from spoiling too quickly. This all begins with removing the guts, and sometimes the skin, from the carcass to preserve the edible areas. Processing is often something that people think will be difficult, but it's pretty simple to figure out what you're doing once you know what you're doing. You just need to know what it will take to make it happen.

The first few times you process something, it might not be pretty, but pretty doesn't matter when it tastes good! The most important thing to remember is to keep your meat clean at all times. This is non-negotiable and will always be the most essential part of the process. Once you've gotten the kill, it's time to clean it to enjoy the fruits of your labor later.

EASY 7 STEP SQUIRREL FIELD DRESSING GUIDE

Squirrels aren't the first animal that people often think of when talking about hunting. They're small and somewhat nutty after a life of eating nuts. In some areas, hunting squirrels is regulated, so make sure that you are always aware of the restrictions placed in your area.

Field dressing squirrels should be done as soon as possible. The animal should be opened up to cool down as soon as it is picked up. Typically, you skin squirrels before you gut them because once you've gutted a squirrel, it doesn't have enough meat to keep it stable enough for the skinning process.

Work in a clean environment as possible to prevent contamination. This will be the first step of every single animal you learn how to dress.

Keep in mind that while traditionally, people create a hole in the hide and pull in opposite directions, because squirrels have tougher hides, they shed hair that gets all over the meat during this process. Instead, you can use a method of skinning that comes with a quick pull. In just seven steps, using a squirrel skinner, you can remove the hide quickly and easily. A squirrel skinner is a piece of metal with three slots where you can put the back legs to skin it easily.

1 Begin by placing the legs in a squirrel skinner, keeping the back facing toward you.

2 Then, remove some of the hair at the base of the tail. This is so you can make a small incision at the base of the tail, cutting between the tail bone joints, then twisting to sever it.

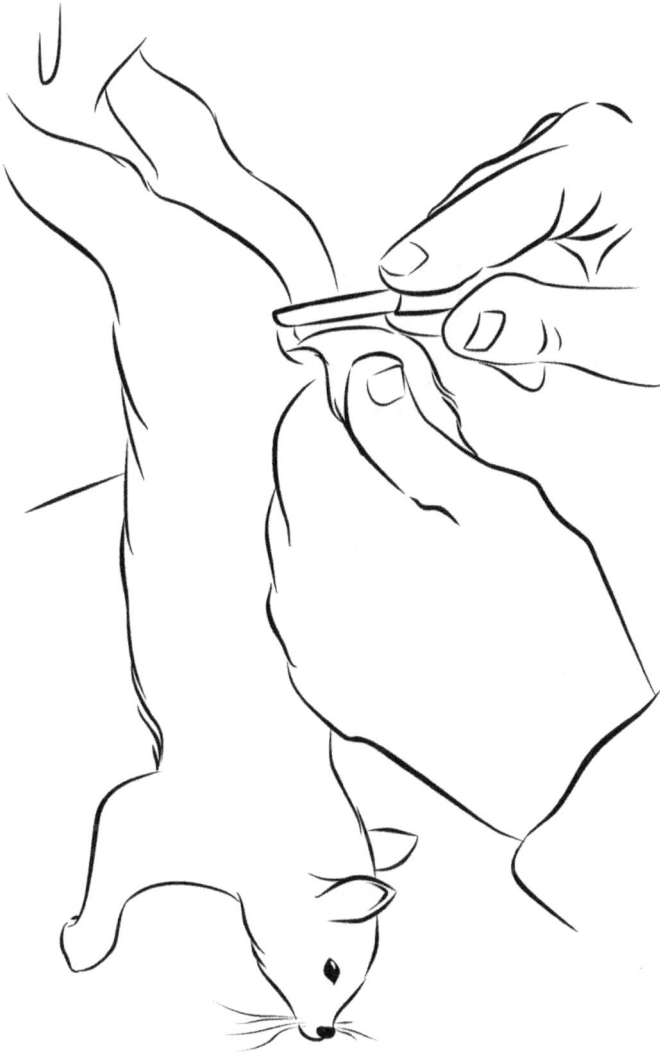

3 Skin down the squirrel's back slowly and carefully for a few inches.

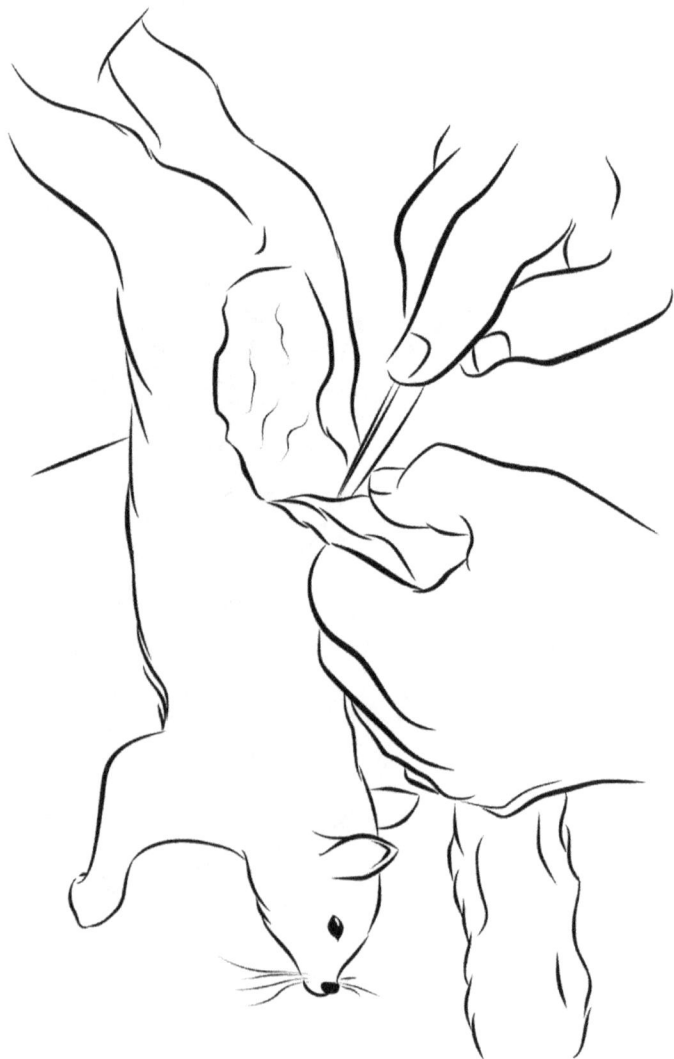

4 Remove the squirrel from the skinner, then grab the back legs. Step down on the tail of the squirrel and pull it up. The front of the hide should then pull down past the front legs.

5 Keeping the tail beneath your foot, hold the skin attached to the belly, and pull it up toward the rear hide past the rear legs.

6 Pull down as far as you can on the hide in the front and rear legs. Most of the heads should be exposed at this point.

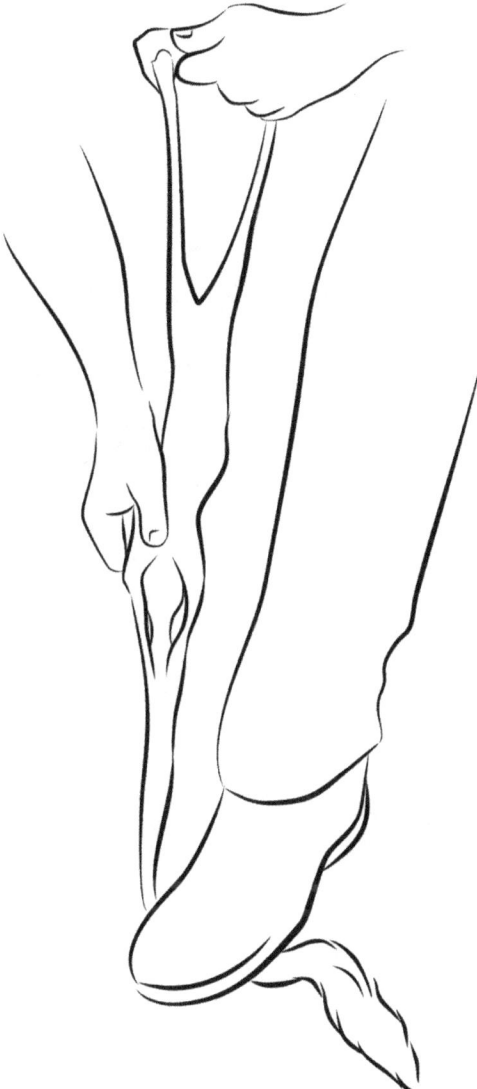

7 Put the squirrel back in the skinner and gut the carcass, then remove the legs with a pair of shears.

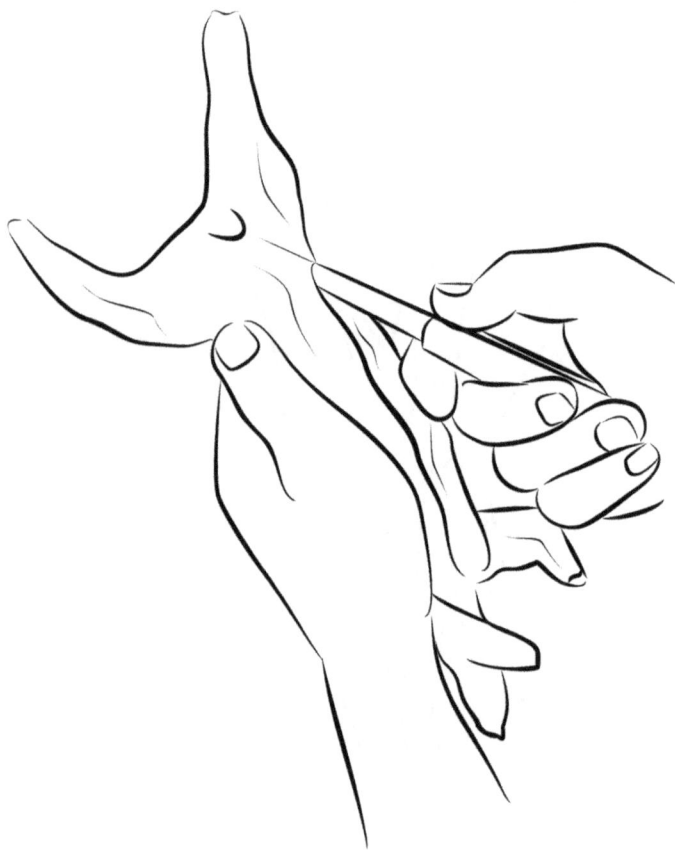

☰ SIMPLE 7 STEP RABBIT FIELD DRESSING GUIDE

Rabbits and hares are easier to handle when compared with squirrels because they're bigger and have more meat on their bones. While squirrels are too delicate to skin after gutting, rabbits are typically field dressed with removing the organs first and then skinning after. Rabbit meat can be a great treat. Wild rabbit is almost chicken-like, sweetish and gamey, and maybe lean as well.

In just seven simple steps, be able to remove everything from your rabbit or hare to have it ready to enjoy it when you want it. You'll need to have game shears, a knife, water, and a garbage bag on hand. And as always, you'll want to remove the skin and field dress it as quickly as possible to cool the meat.

1 Begin by removing the feet at the ankles and the head of your catch.

2 To remove the skin, make a small horizontal cut on the back. Space needs to be enough to insert your fingers and stretch and separate the skin from the meat. Dunk it in the water here.

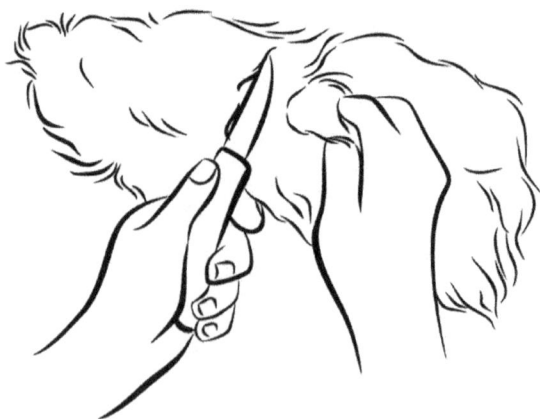

3 From that space, grab the hide at the edge of each slit and pull it down and off. The hide will slide off the animal as you pull at it. The whole thing should come clean.

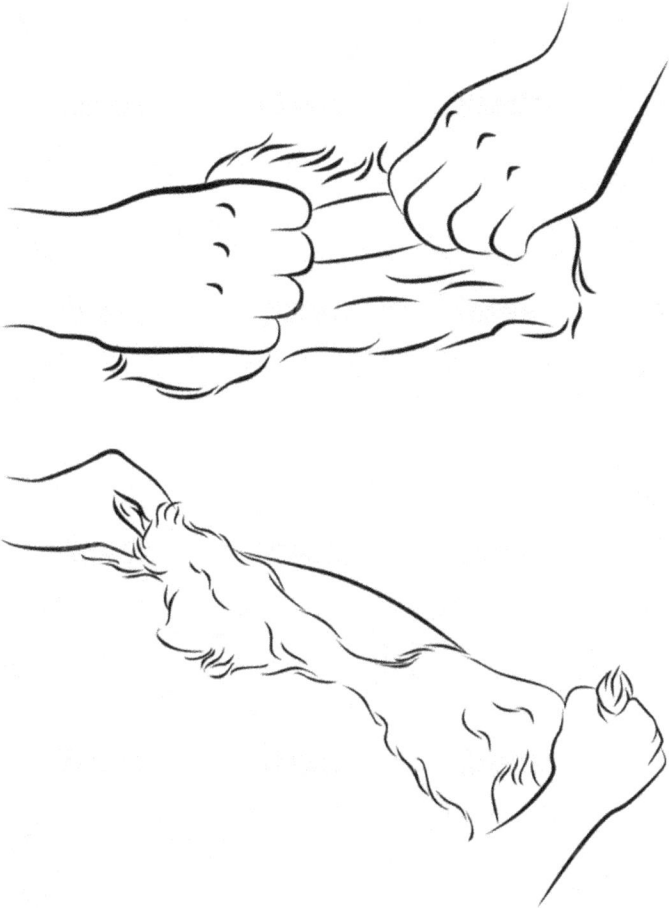

4 Open the belly from the neck to the anus, carefully avoiding the entrails.

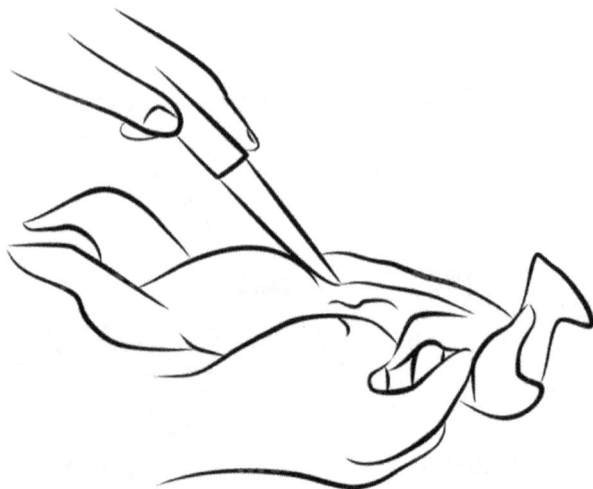

5 Grab the heart and lungs, pulling backward. The entrails should come with it.

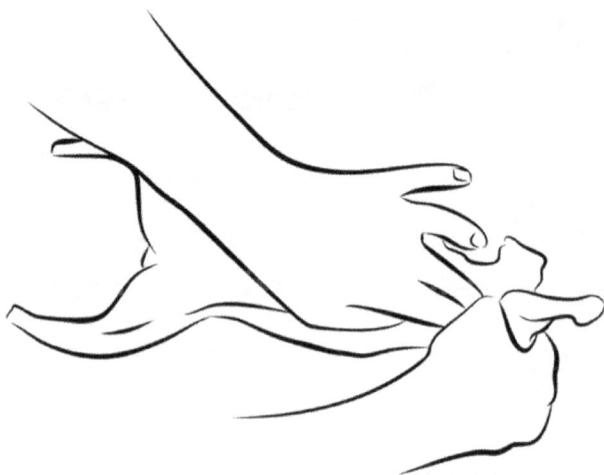

6 Use the knife to remove the hindquarters from the pelvis, front quarters, and backstrap.

7 Finished Piece: Rinse the meat off to remove blood, dirt, and hair, and then either freeze it for later or prepare it for cooking now. You now have a backstrap, thighs, and front legs.

☰ 30 SECOND GROUSE/PARTRIDGE FIELD DRESSING GUIDE

If you haven't had grouse or partridge before, you're in for a treat. They are tender and delicious. If you like poultry, you'll probably like grouse/partridge as well. Cleaning grouse/partridges are incredibly simple. You can do it in seconds when you get good at it, making it highly efficient. All you need to do is ensure that you're on the right track. This method is highly effective for most small game birds.

1 **Place the bird on the ground on its back. Stand on either side of the bird's wings, with the tail end by your heels and the head facing forward. Using your feet to put pressure where the wing joins the body, grab the feet firmly in your hands.**

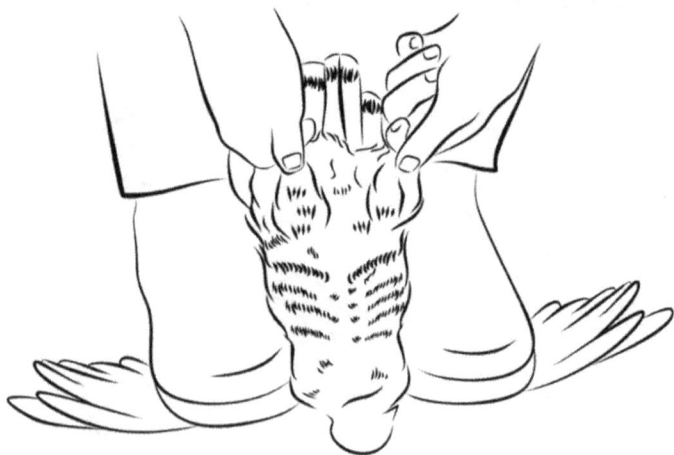

2 Using firm, even pressure, pull the legs up and away from the body. Typically, this is easier with fresher kills. You're then left with the head, entrails, and wings on the ground with the breast while holding the legs in your hand. Use your finger to remove the head and entrails from the breast, starting at the top.

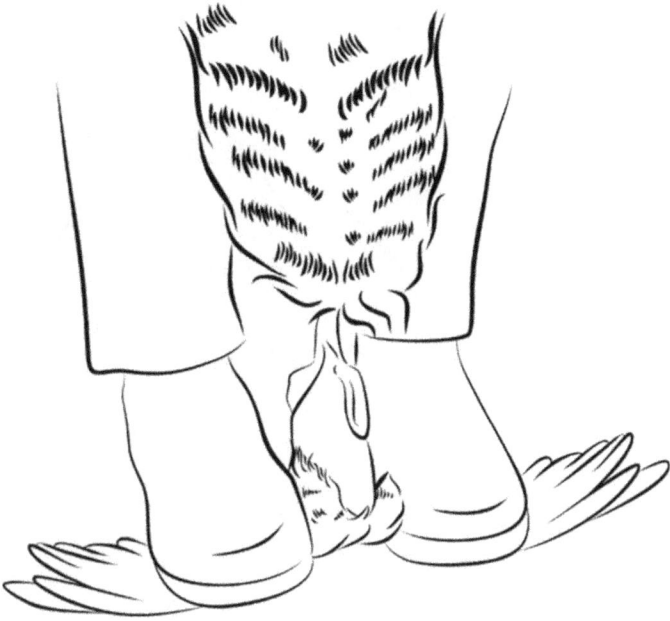

3 Finally, you need to remove the wings. Do so with a sharp knife, or twist and snap them away. Remove any feathers left behind and wash thoroughly under cold running water. Freeze immediately or eat within the next few days.

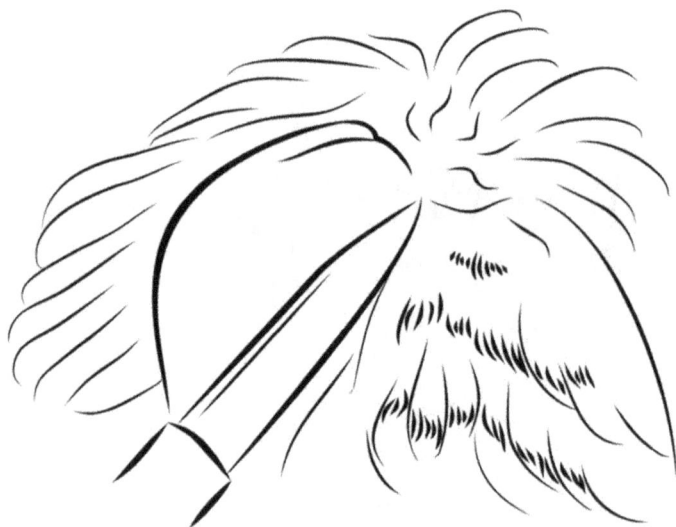

≡ 7-STEP DOVE/PHEASANT/QUAIL FIELD DRESSING GUIDE

Quail can be a great meal if you can find them, but they've slowly become more complex and harder to find. Rather than just breasting the quail, consider removing the feathers, cleaning the birds, and using them whole. You'll be in for a great treat when you do! These birds are pretty small, so you'll want to be mindful of how you use them. Try to make the most out of the meat while you can.

If you've landed a pheasant on the table, you're going to have a delicious meal! The wild pheasant is gamey, aromatic, and lean. They are small, so if you're cooking a meal for several people, you'll probably want a few birds by. It can be a great treat. Keep in mind that in many places, pheasants are regulated, and you are only allowed to hunt males to prevent overhunting or removing valuable females from the reproduction pool.

Alternatively, if you get some dove on the table, you'll have a mild, flavorful meal that may not be as juicy as pheasant but tastes great. This is especially the case if you get morning doves in your area, providing lean, dark meat that tastes amazing.

(Tip: It may be dry, but you can usually keep it moist just by adding bacon. Bacon makes everything delicious!)

Whether you got a dove, pheasant, or quail, the field dressing process is more or less the same. You just have to follow a few simple steps to clean it out and prepare it to eat.

1 Start by removing the head of your bird. This is optional, but ensure that the bird is dead rather than stunned before you move on with the rest of the steps.

2 Next, you need to remove the wings from the bird. The wings and bones are connected to the breast, so you want to ensure they're broken before removal, or you could tear the breast. Grab the bone as close to the body as you can, then twist and snap the wing bone. This will probably rip the skin away as you remove the wing.

3 Take your headless and wingless bird and hold it in your non-dominant hand on its back, with the neck pointing down. Grab the back firmly, with your thumb underneath the base of the tail, as close to the body as you can.

4 Take your dominant hand and use your thumb to find the lip of the breast under the chest. Use your thumbs to push and force their ways through the body cavity, pulling the breast away from the back. The two pieces should hinge near the neck as they separate.

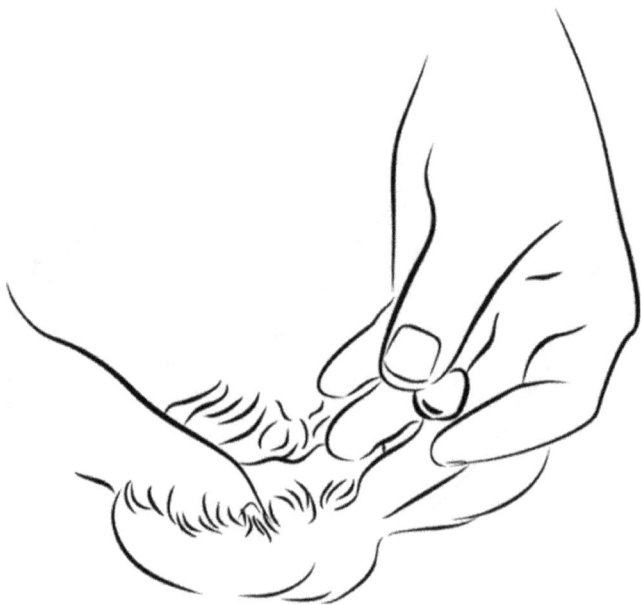

5 You can secure the heart and gizzard, which can provide additional nutrition for you to enjoy. As you pluck these out, slice open the gizzard and remove the liner and the bird's last meal. Clean them up and save them to cook with the bird.

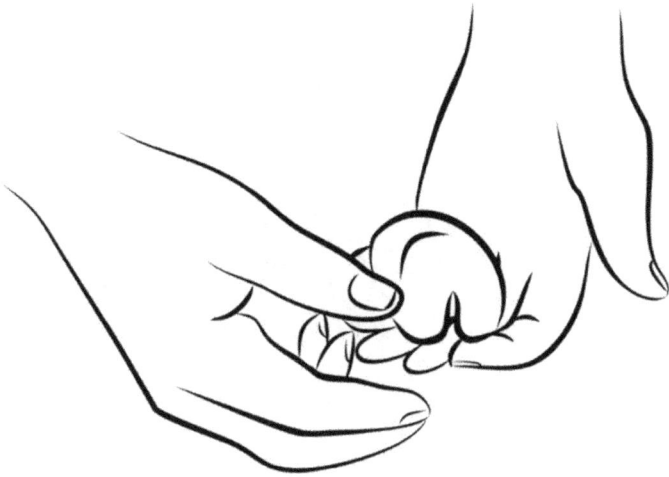

6 Next comes defeathering and removing the breast. You can usually pull the breast away from the rest of the bird easily at this stage, and feathers and skin can be pulled away easily using your fingers.

7 Clean the meat thoroughly at this point and make sure that the meat isn't infested with anything. Worms or infections could taint the meat. Then, cook thoroughly and enjoy. Any extra scraps can bait for future hunts or be disposed of properly.

☰ DUCK

1 Position the duck, so it is on its back, feet directed toward you. With a knife, remove the wings, cutting at the joints to separate them. Pull the wings so you can separate the joint, then cut the connective tissue away.

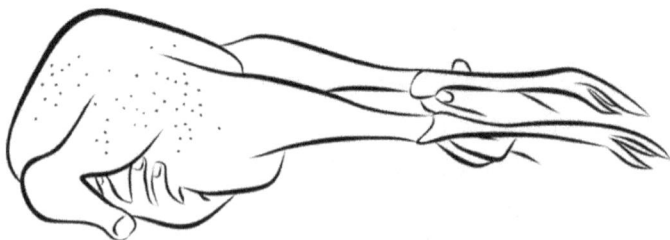

2 Remove the legs by creating an incision all around the large joint, only cutting through the skin. Then, twist the joint a few times to loosen the tendons, remove and pull. The foot should detach with the tendons to create tender thigh meat.

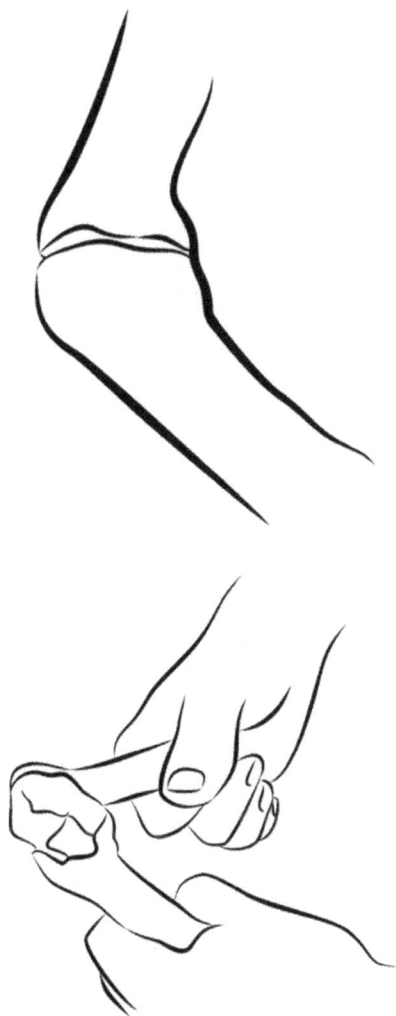

3 Leave the head-on, for now, to hold on to as you pluck feathers. To do so, pinch up a few feathers between your thumb and forefinger, pulling quickly to remove them. Pinch a few at a time to ensure you get cleaner skin without ripping the skin.

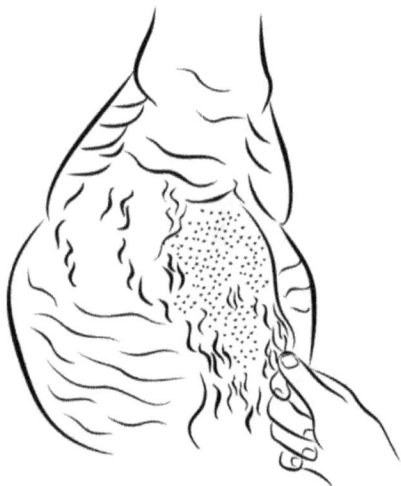

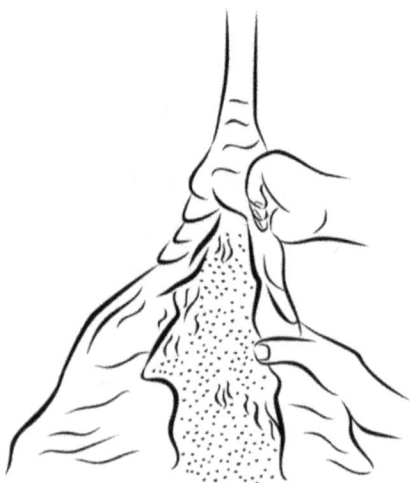

4 When you've removed all the feathers, place the duck down, back up, and tail toward you. Take your knife and create a slit from the base of the back and above the duck's vent. You want to slice through the vertebrae to open the duck. Free the tail and hold the duck, facing up.

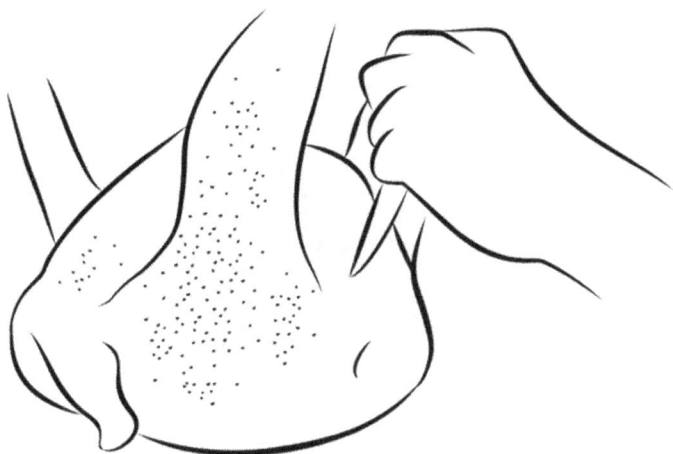

5 Cut carefully, inserting your knife gently into the body cavity, and cut away from you, from the tail end to the neck.

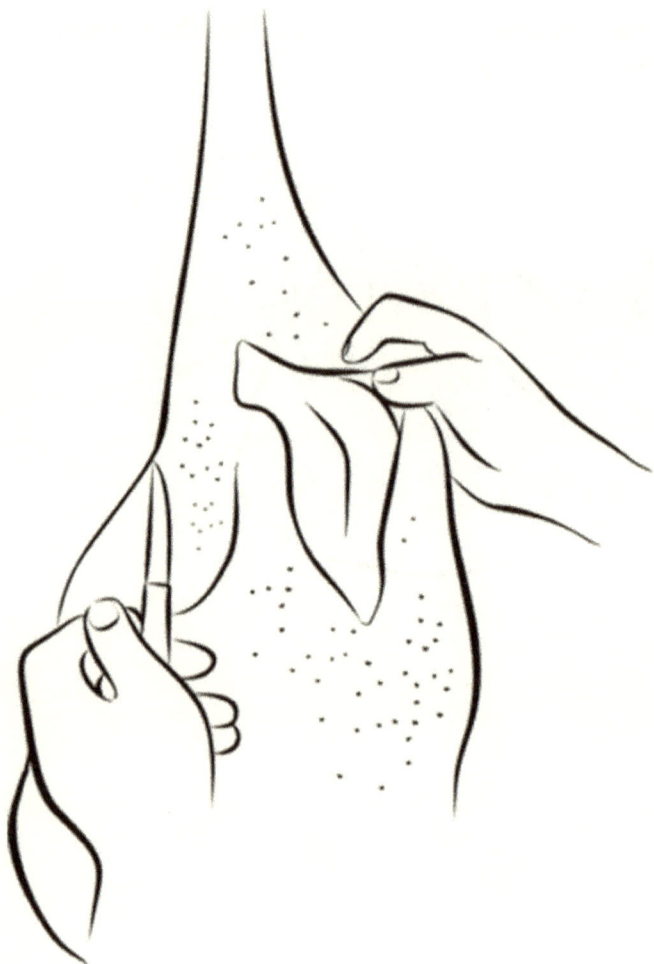

6 Remove the organs now, gently removing them starting at the neck side and working your way down. Start with the windpipe, then the lungs and diaphragm. Loosen the intestines and remove, rinse out the duck, and store until you're ready to eat it.

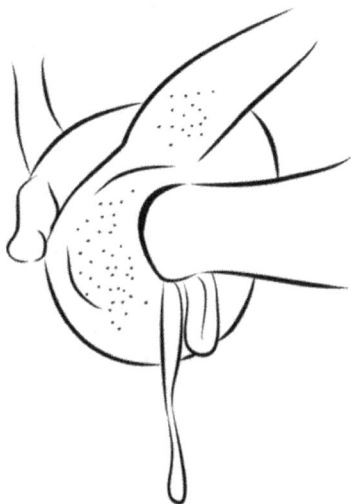

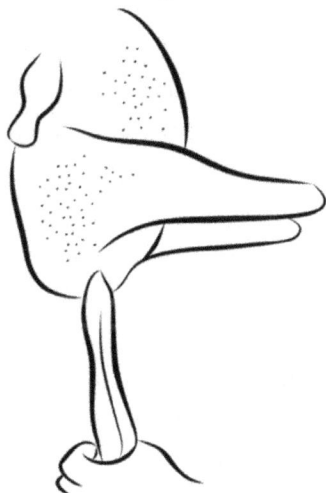

≡ TURKEY/GEESE FIELD DRESSING GUIDE

Wild turkeys in areas like Ontario are a unique breed of animals with distinctive sexual dimorphism that can be readily spotted. However, turkey wasn't always available to hunt. The wild turkey was hunted to extinction in the area and was reintroduced into the wild to repopulate. Because of the shaky status of the birds, hunting is regulated heavily, and people are only allowed to kill a certain amount of wild turkeys, with the annual allowance varying from year to year with the population. Typically, after mating has already passed during spring, male turkeys can be hunted, with females off-limits to encourage an increased population.

It is easy to spot females when hunting. The male wild turkey has black-colored tips on the end of its breast and side feathers, while the females have brown-colored feather tips around its breast and side feathers. The feathers on the chest of the male turkey are also longer than those on the female body, and the male turkeys make a lot more noise than their female counterparts. The male wild turkey is called a tom, while the female is known as a hen.

Many hunters advocate for keeping the skin on these birds—removing it is to remove delicious fat and flavor that can crisp up into something extraordinary if you let it cook. When you take care of a large bird, the first step is to pluck first before gutting, as otherwise, you may struggle to clean around the incision. Follow these simple steps.

1. Start by hanging your bird up by the neck. This will give you access to the whole thing all around, allowing the next several steps to be much easier.

2. Slowly remove the feathers, just a few at a time, tugging up and away from the bird to get them out of the skin.

3. Be mindful not to tear the skin, especially near the breast. It is the most fragile there, and you want the breast skin intact if you intend to roast your bird whole.

4. Continue to pluck, mindful that the most difficult parts will be the wing bones and the armpit area beneath the wing.

5. When you've removed all the feathers, you can then gut the bird entirely. Doing so while it's still hanging makes it easier. Create the gutting incision at the cloaca, and then slice toward the point of the breastbone.

6. Reach your hand into the cavity, pushing your hand to the windpipe. You'll need a firm grasp to bring the guts out without spilling their contents.

7. Keep the heart, liver, and gizzard.

8. Then, remove the breast sponge on turkeys. This is a collection of fatty tissue that sits above the breastbone and underneath the crop. To remove this, you'll need to cut up each side of the wishbone through the skin.

9. Next, slice the sack of fat away and leave behind the clean meat.

10. Remove the bird's head next. The wings can be left if you've completely plucked them. If they're not fully plucked, make sure you leave at least the first major joint intact, and you can cut beyond that, as there's very little usable meat in the second and third pieces of the wing, anyway.

11. Remove the legs, cutting around the joint where the rubbery scales meet the skin.

12. Snap the joint in half, and it should crack like a stick. Then, cut the tendons free. It's better to snap and remove the joint this way as sharp pieces of bone can pierce vacuum-seal bags if you decide to break down your kill further.

1 MINUTE BULLFROG FIELD DRESSING GUIDE

Many people don't hunt bullfrogs. However, other people simply don't like the idea of eating them, but they're missing out! These can be delicious meals that most people overlook. They're commonly served in restaurants in the south, France, Asia, and just about anywhere else where frogs can be found. However, especially the West Coast of the US has overlooked this delicious opportunity for plentiful meals.

Bullfrogs are invasive species in many places, so hunting them does the native species a favor. Once you've caught and killed a frog, you can then gut and clean it, enjoying the delicious meat. Most of the meat is found in the legs, so usually, people forgo worrying about the rest of them. The skin doesn't taste very good either, so you'll want to remove it.

Before you get started, you'll want to have a few tools on hand—shears, pliers, water, a sharp knife, and somewhere to dispose of the scraps left behind. Then, you can follow these steps.

1 Begin by removing the feet. It's easier to skin them when this is done.

2 Slice the skin around the frog's waist. You can use either the kitchen shears or the knife, depending on what works best for you.

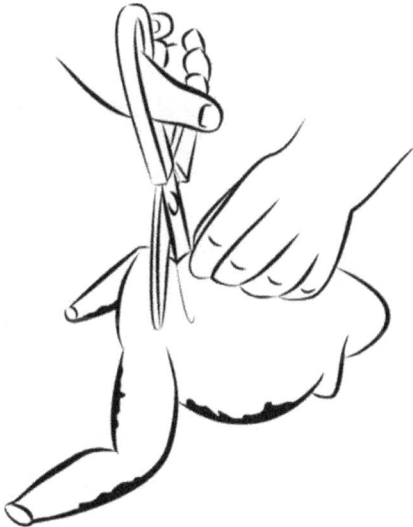

3 When the skin's been cut all the way around, the next step is easy. You'll use one hand to hold the top of the frog firmly. Then, take the pliers to grab the loose skin and yank the skin off, like you're pulling off a pair of pants.

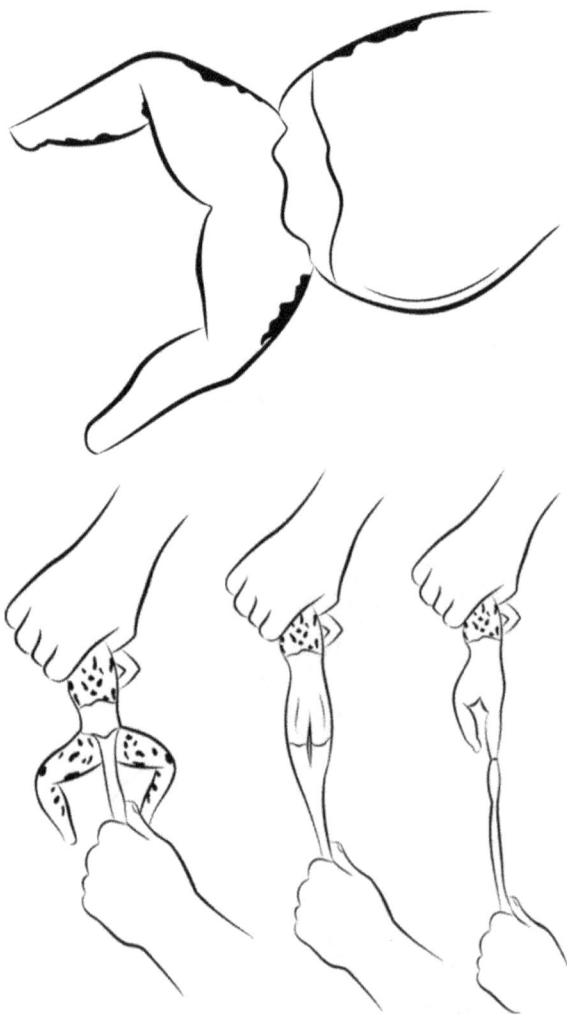

4 With the skin removed, use a pair of shears to chop off the legs like a pair right at the waist. Then, chop again to separate the legs into two pieces. You can also trim off any bits that look like organs kept on the leg slide when cutting.

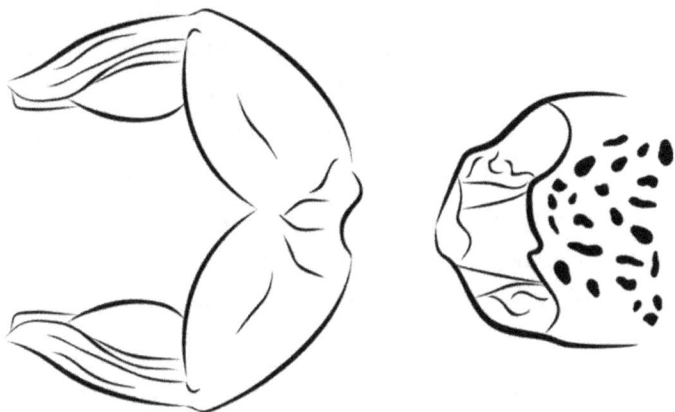

☰ SNAPPING TURTLE FIELD DRESSING GUIDE

If you get your hands on a snapping turtle (preferably the tail end so it can't bite you!), you've got a delicious meal, especially if you tenderize it and enjoy it in a delicious recipe. When you catch a snapping turtle, you're able to eat something tasty that most people will never bother enjoying. It's almost like being part of an exclusive club, knowing that everyone else is missing out because it's not traditionally eaten anymore.

Snapping turtles can be difficult to skin simply because they've got that massive shell on them, but if you can learn to do so effectively, you'll be in for a treat, and if you live somewhere, these are plentiful, you'll have even more to enjoy. Follow these simple steps to prepare your own.

1 **Start by finding a snapper yourself. You'll be able to do this in the wild if they're native to your area. Just keep them by their tail end to keep yourself safe. They pack quite a punch or, rather, bite.**

2 When you've got your turtle, stand on its shell to hold it in place to smash the head inwards toward the shell. This stuns the turtle so you can then continue the process. To kill it, you'll need to remove its head, slicing from the throat, through the spine, and then remove the head. This quickly kills it.

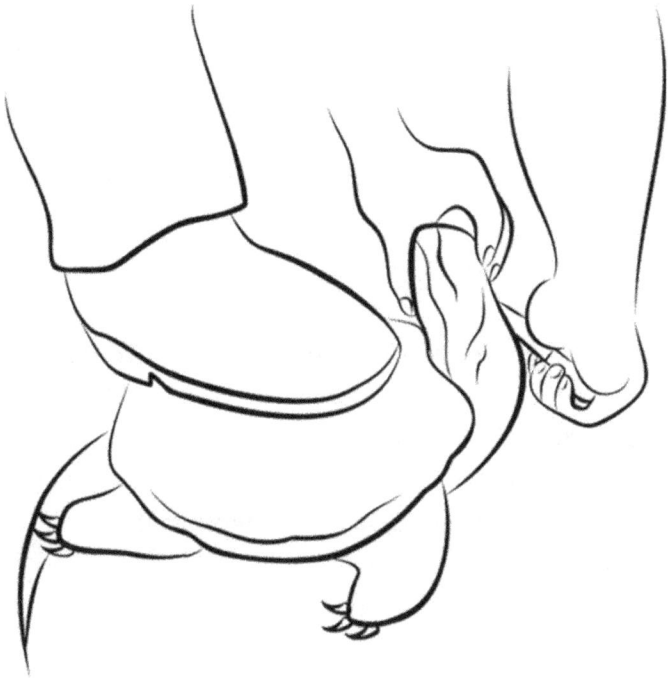

3 The easiest way to clean the turtle is to have it held in place. Prepare a plank of wood with a long nail through the center. Then, with the point of the nail through the wood and facing up, drive the turtle onto the nail to hold it in place. Start by removing the feet. You'll find the joints an inch behind the claws.

4 Next, you need to remove the shell. To do this, you'll need to cut through the center of the plate to the vent. Use a sharp, strong knife, plus a wooden baton if necessary to push it through. Cut down the center, then cut the perimeter to remove it.

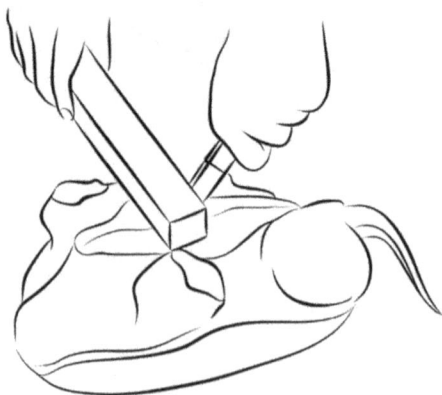

5 Start skinning the turtle from the inside out. Be mindful when you start because the front shoulder blade is near the shell. You don't want to cut too quickly and have your knife rebound out. Let the knife feel its way through slowly as you go.

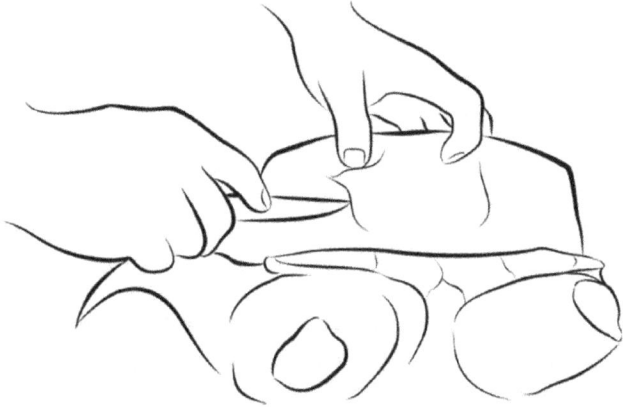

6 Then work around the legs to remove the skin. When the skin is removed, use a knife to remove the feet, slicing through the line under the shell and pulling it off.

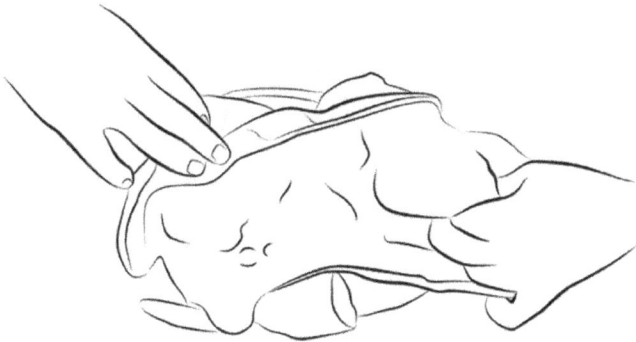

7 Pull-on, the tail, using the knife to remove the meat from the backbone.

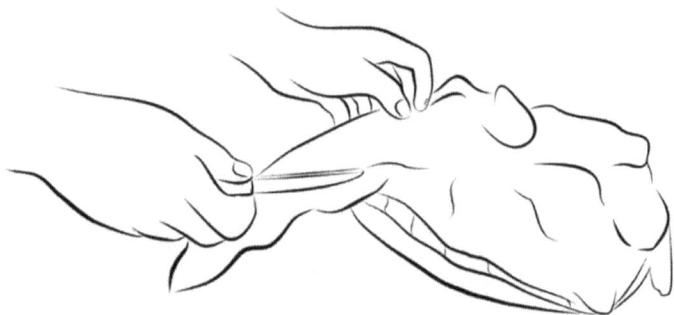

8 Pull out the meat as you cut. You may also find eggs as you do so, and those are edible as well.

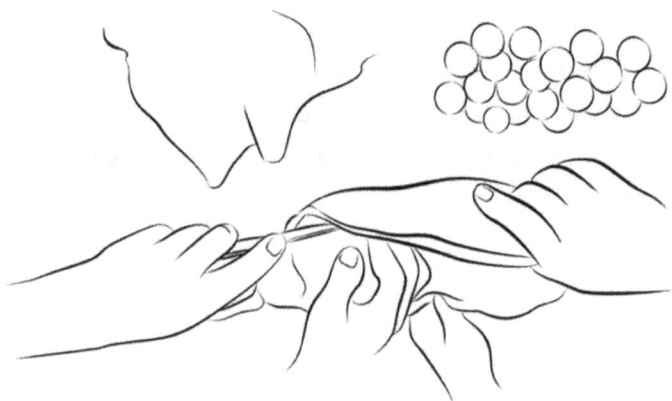

9 Finish scraping all meat out.

10 Meat can be broken down further or deboned if desired. Soak in water overnight for a day or two before cooking.

11 **Finished Product:**

6 STEP FISH FILLET GUIDE

Filleting a fish that you've caught is simple, and the meat often tastes so much better than anything you can get from a supermarket. There's nothing better than enjoying something that you caught and butchered on your own. Following a few simple steps on how to fillet fish will go a long way. In just six steps, you can have your fish ready to eat.

1 **The first step is to make an incision from the bottom of the gills to the spine.**

2 **Start by removing the head. To do so, place your knife behind the pectoral fin and cut diagonally downward to get through the bone. Repeat this on the other side as well and remove and discard the head.**

3 Next, remove the tail, using your knife to cut where the tail fin joins the body. Cut straight down through the flesh and bone, then discard the fin.

4 Begin at the head end. Use a fillet knife to run along the backbone in as smooth of a motion as possible. It might take over one cut, depending on how large the fish is. You'll want to cut around the ribcage to release the fillet.

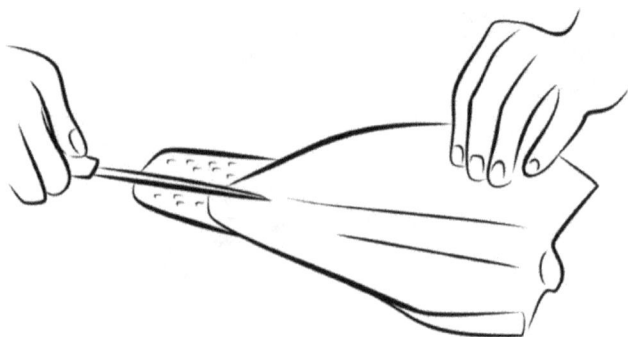

5 Trimming comes next. You'll want to cut the thin belly portion off. While it tastes good and is acceptable, you can enjoy another aspect to cook. You can enjoy another factor that will cook quicker because it is so much thinner. Reserve it to cook separately, or use it for stock instead of cooking it with the fillet.

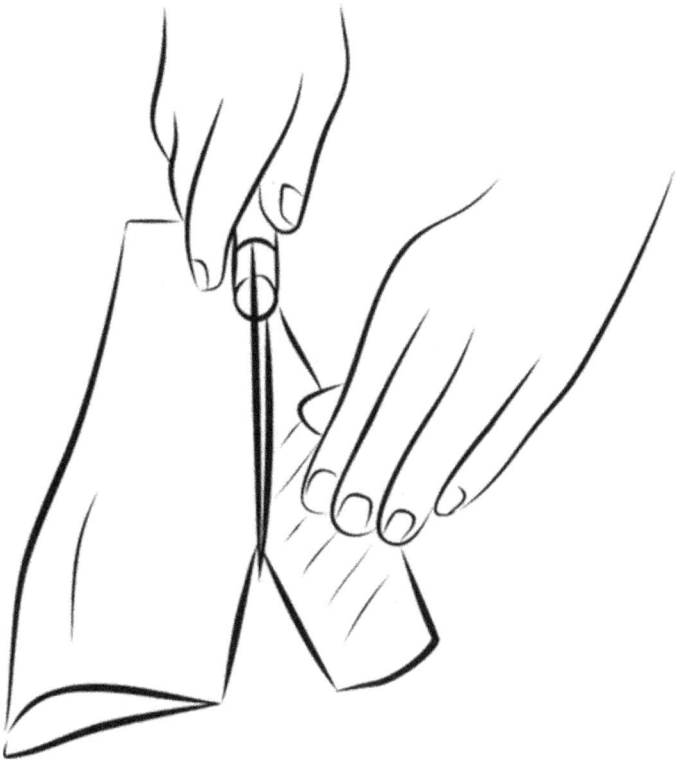

6 Finally, remove the skin. Keep the skin side down, then put your knife at the tail end, situating the blade between the flesh and skin. Use the knife to slowly run along the fillet, tipping the knife downward slightly to avoid cutting into the flesh. The whole fillet should come off and will be ready to cook.

5

SKINNING IS WINNING

While you may hunt primarily to enjoy the food, another aspect that you can enjoy is skinning to mount the hide. Using taxidermy is an excellent way to collect trophies, especially if you have a perfect specimen. Sometimes, an animal can look too good to waste, or you want it as a souvenir.

When you are skinning small game, you need to be mindful of the knife that you choose. Fixed blades that can be sharpened are usually preferred, as they will last longer, but if you're carrying along with a knife as you hunt, you may need to consider getting a folding one. Either way, keep in mind that your blade will need to be small, precise, and extremely sharp. Sharp and precise will ensure that you're able to get the cut in and control it to the best of your ability.

Even if you're just trying to get the skin, it's important to recognize that preparation must happen. You can't usually just leave the animal intact until you can get it to a taxidermist. Instead, field prep as carefully as possible. There are a few essential rules to remember to ensure you have beautiful, intact skins to create beautiful trophies:

1. The carcass still must remain cool. Especially if you are hunting somewhere warm, you want to keep it cool if you're not skinning it immediately.

2. Be delicate with small game and birds. While you might not see the harm in carrying a bird by its neck, you may deform the skin while doing so. You also should not allow dogs to retrieve small game you intend to mount.

3. Cut carefully: always avoid cutting the neck or chest when you do any field dressing beforehand. We'll go over a few simple skinning guides shortly to help you field dress effectively.

4. Ask for tips from your taxidermist. If you have one that you work with exclusively, ask them what they want you to do before bringing the animal to them. Some will have different preferences than others. By acknowledging their preferences before you begin, you up the chances of a successful and beautifully life like mount. As you read over this chapter, you will be introduced to a few key topics. We will go over how to skin squirrels, rabbits, and birds for taxidermy. Then, we will address how to tan hides to prepare them for taxidermy. These topics should provide a cursory introduction to anything that you may need to know for your taxidermy.

HOW TO SKIN SMALL GAME FOR THE FUR

If you want an animal's fur for any reason, whether as a trophy mount, to make other items lined with fur, or for any other reasons, you will need to remove it without damaging it significantly and then treat it. Hence, it's ready to be tanned. Upon removing the skin from an animal, there will still be veins and arteries attached to the skin. There will still be a membrane that you will have to remove as well. We will address skinning squirrels for taxidermy, skinning a rabbit pelt, and skinning birds for trophies. From there, the next section will address how to treat and tan the hide.

SKINNING SQUIRRELS FOR TAXIDERMY

Skinning squirrels for taxidermy differs from the skin for food. Skinning for food is all about getting the skin off completely and quickly to get the rest of the meat ready to cook. Skinning for a mount requires precision and attention to detail that otherwise wouldn't matter. It is crucial that, while skinning, you take your time to be as gentle as possible or you could damage the skin relatively easily. The skin isn't as tough as you might think!

1. First incision: The first incision is done at the top with dorsal skinning. This is a favorite for taxidermists as it is a single cut along the spine that requires minimal sewing. Start just behind the shoulders, then cut down to before the hips. Then, you can carefully work the inner membrane along the sides away from the skin

with your fingers. If the squirrel is still warm, this is easy.

2. The hind legs: To remove the skin from the hind legs, you must work with your fingers to loosen the skin around the hind legs. Push the knee until you can see the joint, then carefully work it down. It should peel off pretty easily. Once you've arrived at the ankle joint, you can use the knife's tip to remove tendons and ligaments connected to the foot bones. Be mindful that tugging too much or cutting a bit too far might destroy the foot's skin. Do so until you get to the toe bones. When you're at the toes, clip the joints connected to the bones, and the skin should detach completely. Repeat this for the other leg.

3. Stripping the tail: The tail is especially tricky to remove, but if it tears, you may salvage it by sewing it together, but do the best you can to detach it in one piece. When both hind legs are out, you can grasp the base of the tailbone and the base of the tail skin with your fingers. Then, pull the bone out. Hold the skin in place without pulling it at all as the bones slip out. They should come out in one piece, leaving you with an empty tail. Gently move the hind end of the pelt toward the shoulders.

4. Skinning the front legs: Next, work on the front legs. These are skinned, similar to the hind legs. Work the skin off with your fingers to the ankle. Use your knife to loosen tendons and ligaments, and snip at the toe bones.

5. Skinning the ears: With the front legs free, you can now start detaching the skin from the head. Pull the skin forward over the neck like removing a shirt, gently continuing until you get to the cartilage of the ears. You will notice these as little pale lumps on the head. Using your knife as carefully as possible, remove the cartilage, cutting toward the skull to protect the skin. With the ear bases free, you can pull further until you arrive at the back sections of the eyes, which will look like dark, blue areas from underneath the skin.

6. Skinning the eyes and mouth: Carefully remove the membrane connecting the corner of the eye to the skull, leaving the eyelids intact on the hide. Do this on the other side and peel the skin until it arrives at the edge of the mouth. Cut the membrane connecting the mouth to the skin and continue peeling to the nose. Use a pair of scissors to cut the nose cartilage away from the skull. The skin is now completely removed. This process maintains the feet, toes, claws, whiskers, eyelids, and nose, which means it's ready to tan. If you're not ready to tan or take it to a taxidermist, you can turn it right side out and freeze it in a Ziploc bag until you're ready to use it.

SKINNING RABBITS FOR THEIR PELTS

Rabbits are commonly recognized for their beautiful pelts that can be used widely. In this tutorial, you will be left with a pelt that can be lining for hats or gloves or in any other manner you'd like.

1. Removing the ankles: Start by slicing around all ankle joints, then twist to break the bone and remove them.

2. Creating a belly incision: Carefully, to not penetrate the guts, make a quick slit in the loose belly skin. It helps pinch a piece of skin in the lower abdomen, pull away from the body, and then slit to make an opening.

3. Loosening skin: Use a finger to loosen the belly skin from the body. When it is loose enough, insert your knife and extend the incision. Repeat this process into the chest. You should now have a slit from the bottom belly to the chest.

4. Loosening skin from the body: Gently using your hands, separate the skin from the sides of the body and the back.

5. Remove back legs from the skin: With the skin loosened, be able to slip your finger around the hind leg's knee joint from the inside. Pull the knee inward, and it should slide out of the skin. Repeat on the other leg and loosen the skin around the rear of the rabbit.

6. Free lower skin: Detach the skin from the anus, carefully avoiding cutting the skin. Then, pull the skin away from the tail until you can make a clean cut across the tailbone.

7. Pulling skin from the body: Holding the skin by the legs, pull the skin up to the neck. Work the skin off of the front legs in the same manner you removed the rear legs. Then pull the skin up and over the head. It should break off, leaving the skin around the head while you have a complete pelt.

☰ SKINNING BIRDS FOR TAXIDERMY

Most birds can be skinned similarly to get a proper hide that you can then mount. Whether you've got a turkey, duck, or quail, there's a good chance that you can use this method to remove the skin to prepare for a taxidermist.

1. The incision: Like with a squirrel, you want to create an incision in the back, which can be hidden well and easily sewn up after a taxidermist has finished working on it. The incision on a bird will begin on the back, right before the head begins. Do your best to part feathers to avoid cutting any in half, and try not to get the feathers wet or they will get sticky. The incision should go from the base of the tail to the head.

2. Separating skin from the body: The next thing to do is to separate the skin from either side of the body. Peel gently toward the wings. This is easiest if the body is warm. Try to keep the innards and skin wet underneath, careful not to get any water on the feathers.

3. Separate the skin from the head: Carefully separate the skin from the rest of the bird, grabbing the neck (not pulling on it). Cut the neck from the body, carefully avoiding cutting the skin. After cutting the neck off from the body, cut off as much of the inner neck as possible. Use tweezers to pull out the brains and eyes carefully. You have a bird with the skin removed from the body with the neck removed and the head emptied.

4. Finishing skinning: Gently remove the skin from around the legs, breaking bones attached to the thighs. You can break the bones off at the thigh, leaving them in the lower part of the foot and the feet. Just make sure there is as little meat as possible left behind.

5. Skinning the wings: To remove the wings, break them off where they attach to the body. They will dry out with the skin.

6. Peeling the skin: Now, beginning at the neck, you can gently remove the skin, careful to avoid making any holes in it.

7. Snipping the tail: The tail will still be attached to the body at this point. You can remove it by carefully snipping off the tail bone, leaving as much meat attached to the body (and away from the skin) as possible. Your skin is now ready to take to a taxidermist.

☰ TANNING SKINS

If you want to tan your pelt yourself, you can do so. If it's a furred animal, you can wash the skin in cold water while finishing the field dressing. This is primarily to keep the skin fresh while removing any leftover fur or blood from the fur. Wash the skin with a mild soap (unnecessary, but can help if you prefer). Get all the blood off the skin. Then, gently squeeze it when you remove it from the water. Don't wring it out, which can stretch or damage the skin. Let the hide dry out overnight.

(Tip: Dawn soap is the best. Suitable for cleaning contaminants off of animals too!)

To let it dry well, you can nail the hides to a plank of wood, nailing one corner down at a time. This stretches them out while they drive. Make sure the nails aren't deep; they should pop out with a hammer when pried.

The hides must now be treated for use. There is a layer of the membrane inside of the hide that needs to be removed. It should peel off relatively easily. Try to get as much off as possible. Then, it's time for treatment. A good treatment is a soak in water, salt, and borax.

The hide's inner layer should be coated with a thick layer of salt. This salt should be deep enough to coat the whole thing. Make sure there is no hide left showing through it. This will remove moisture out and cure the hide, so it does not rot. Add more salt every day or two. You can keep the hides nailed down to prevent shrinkage or leave them down flat. They need salt as long as they still have moisture. They should feel completely dry when it's time to work them over.

When they're completely dry, you can start working them over. You will use your hands to blend them until they become pliable. Be gentle during this process. The skin will take some time to be worked through completely. Once the skin has been worked through, it's ready to use for just about anything you'd like.

6

PRACTICAL COOKING AND PREPARING YOUR SMALL GAME

Preparing your meat might be pretty intimidating at first. It's hard to know what to do when you've never done it before. However, the first time is the hardest—and it gets easier every time you do it from there! Eating your harvest is perhaps the most satisfying part of the entire process—you're getting to enjoy something that will be delicious, and you provided it for yourself.

As you read through this chapter, you will get a basic introductory guide to each common small game meat you may have hunted for yourself. We'll go over the most common way to butcher up the meat once it's been skinned and field dressed, how to store it effectively, and some of the basic tips for preparing the food in a tasty manner. This chapter is a precursor to the next chapter, emphasizing several delicious recipes using these different meats to enjoy. As you read this chapter, you'll learn about how these meats taste and what they pair well with, so you can also start thinking of your ways that you may prefer to prepare these meats.

Keep in mind that some of these meats may have gained tastes—if you've grown up eating processed foods and supermarket meat, you may not be accustomed to the gamey taste many of these different meats have. They are earthier or even somewhat iron-like. However, if you gain the taste for it or simply enjoy gaminess already, you will find these highly satisfying. After all, what's more satisfying, than living off the land, as we did before we had civilization? What's more satisfying than getting back to your roots and being self-sustaining? And, what's better than knowing exactly where that meat came from and how it was processed? You don't get these benefits from ordering from the supermarket—you get it from growing or hunting your meat. These are important life skills that are crucial to know in case of an emergency.

SQUIRREL

Butchering Squirrel

Once you have the hair removed, you can remove the head, the feet, and the guts. Save the liver, heart, and kidneys. Then, use a pair of scissors to split the pelvis and remove the anus. Wash well and then break down the squirrel.

Begin by removing the legs. Then, slice down the ribcage to behind the front leg. Cut along the bones toward the neck until the forelegs are free, leaving a skinny collarbone behind. The hind legs can be removed by slicing the meat inside the squirrel's leg, right where it is attached to the body. When you see the ball joint, bend the leg and pop the joint out, then slice the remaining meat and connective tissue to free it. Do so for both legs.

Use the kitchen shears to remove the ribs and save them for stock if you'd like. Use shears or a cleaver to remove the hips and the neck, and you're left with the backstrap. The scraps of meat and skeleton can be used for stock.

Storing Squirrel

Butchered squirrels can be preserved by freezing in a vacuum-sealed bag. The rabbit should be refrigerated for 24- 36 hours before freezing until the meat is not rigid. Then, it can be frozen. It may also be pressure canned.

Tips for Cooking Squirrel

Squirrel tastes sweet and nutty, somewhere between chicken and rabbit. To enjoy it, consider braising or slow-cooking it, so it is tender and juicy. It can also be used in most chicken recipes.

☰ RABBIT

Butchering Rabbit

Butchering a rabbit is a little more complicated than butchering a chicken but can be done relatively quickly. When the skin and guts have been removed, you can begin preparing the meat for consumption.

Begin by trimming any sinew or silverskin that's left behind on the carcass. Then, remove the front legs. They aren't attached to the body by bone, so they should come off easily. All you need to do is slide the knife up from underneath, going along the ribs, and then slice through it. Remove any sinew or ligaments from the front legs and set them aside.

Remove the belly next. Carefully cut right along the beginning of the loin, and then cut along the edge of the ribs, filleting the meat off the ribs. Trim any inedible bits off and set the belly strips aside.

Remove the hind legs. These can make up about 40% of the total weight. Begin on the bottom side, gently slicing along the pelvis until you can see the ball and socket joint. Hold either side firmly, bending back to pop the joint out. Then, you finish cutting the meat to free the leg. Do this on both sides.

Remove the loin. Begin by removing the silverskin. There are likely several layers on the back to be removed. Remove the pelvis (it can make broth later). Then, use kitchen shears to cut the ribs off the meat (ribs can go in the broth as well). Remove any more silverskin, then portion the loin into suitable serving sizes.

Storing Rabbit

The rabbit should be frozen if you're not using it within 24 hours of butchering. Store it in the freezer in vacuum-sealed bags for between 9-12 months. It can be thawed in the fridge for 1-2 days before using it.

Tips for Cooking Rabbit

Rabbit meat is like a gamy chicken. It's dryer, with a bit of an earthy taste to it. Removing all the silverskin prevents tough sinew from being present on the meat. Rabbit can be cooked in just about any way you could think of; braised, baked, roasted, and stewed are all perfectly acceptable. You can also bread and fry it.

☰ GROUSE

Grouse is known for its richly red meat with a deep, intense flavor. Ideally, you would have younger birds for quick cooking methods and older birds for slow cooking to tenderize them. To tell, look at the feet. Sharper claws and flexible breast bones typically imply younger birds.

Butchering Grouse

If you have field dressed a grouse by stepping on the wings and pulling the feet, you're left with a breast and wings. From there, you must separate the breast from the bones to prepare them for use. Remember that many places require you to keep a wing on the breast for identification while hunting, so know your local regulations.

When ready to use, twist and pull the wings off.

From there, when it's time to remove the meat from the bone, you can use a kitchen knife to carefully separate the breast from the bone, following the breastbone. Ensure there are no feathers, dirt, or bone left in the meat, and you're ready to cook.

Storing Grouse

Make sure the grouse meat is stored carefully. The best way to do so is to wrap the meat with wax paper and then vacuum seal it in a bag. However, they taste the best fresh.

Tips for Cooking Grouse

Before you begin, always cut out the shot that was used to kill the bird. Also, make sure that any extra feathers are removed. Heavily bloody areas should also be removed. Trussing the bird will help it keep its shape as you cook.

Pair grouse with fruit jelly, some game chips, and gravy. Blackberries and beetroots are common flavors.

PARTRIDGE

Butchering Partridge

If you want to roast a whole partridge, you may not want to separate the breast from the wings in the traditional field dressing method that involves tearing the wings and breast from the bottom. Butchering the partridge for use isn't that difficult on its own, though feather removal may take a while.

Begin by removing the feathers from the body and legs. Then, you will want to remove the head, the wings, and the legs at the natural bend. You can remove the legs well by nicking the bend in the ankle, then twisting and pulling out all the tendons from the leg.

To gut, you can lift the anal vent and make a small incision to fit two fingers in, Carefully scrape out the innards, trying not to burst any guts. Flip over the birds and cut along the neckbone to remove the neck, leaving as much meat as possible.

You can leave a slit in the bottom near the tail, which you can use to keep the legs in place by sticking the bottom of the legs into the hole to keep them tucked in before using a truss to keep them close. Then, it's ready to prepare.

Storing Partridge

It's recommended that to store the partridge well, you wrap it with cling film, then use a vacuum sealer. If you're saving feathered meat, you can wrap it in newspaper first, then cling film, and then vacuum seal. It's usually better to prepare the meat to oven-ready states, remove bloodied meat, and ensure it's ready to go when it's thawed. Try to use it within six months, though it should still be suitable for 12.

Tips for Cooking Partridge

Make sure that you remove any damaged meat, a lead that may be left behind from killing. It's not always possible to have perfectly nice meat when hunting, so don't worry too much if you don't land the kill shot in the head. You can just trim off bloodied pieces, and there's a good chance the meat itself will be fine.

☰ DOVE

Butchering Dove

Dove's breasts are the primary part that is eaten. You can do so easily, removing the wings with a pair of butchering shears. Then, use your thumbs to tear the skin across the breast.

Remove the crop (the pouch with the last meal) from the breast and pull away.

Make snips at the bottom of the breast going up one direction, then the other. You've separated much of the breast from the body. Use your hands to pull off the breast on the bone and trim off the wing joints. You've now got a breast attached to the breastbone, and you can discard the rest.

Wash well to remove blood and feathers. To remove the breast from the breastbone, you can use a knife to cut along the bottom of the breastbone, trimming to the keel but not separating it. Then, work along with the others. The breast is now freed up to the keel, and you can gently detach it from the keel and use it.

Storing Dove

Doves can be stored wrapped in cling film and vacuum sealed. If you don't have a vacuum sealer, you can also use freezer bags with the dove and some water to cover up the meat to prevent freezer burning.

Tips for Cooking Dove

Dove is dry and benefits well from using bacon or some other fatty source to keep some moisture. A great way to prepare them is to wrap them in bacon, stick with a toothpick (or stuff with other ingredients if you want to), and fry up quickly. Keep in mind these breasts are small, so that you may need several for a meal.

PHEASANT

Butchering Pheasant

As a larger bird, the pheasant can offer several pieces of meat that can be enjoyed. You will butcher it predominantly the same way you would butcher a chicken, leaving you with eight cuts of two legs, two thighs, two breasts, and two wings.

Begin by disjointing the legs and thighs from the pheasant by cutting in until you've reached the joint. You can use the knife to loosen the flesh around the joint, then twist and pull it to pop it out of the socket. Do this on both sides.

To separate the breast meat, have the pheasant resting on its back and cut close to the sternum, following down where the breast will meet the wing. Do so on both sides. You should have breasts, wings, and leg quarters at this point.

Now, separate between the leg and thigh. The point will be noticeable because of the fat left there. Use the fat as the guide and cut through the piece.

Storing Pheasant

To store pheasant, butcher it down to the form you would like to use it. Then, store wrapped in cling film and then sealed in vacuum-sealed bags.

Tips for Cooking Pheasant

Pheasant can be used instead of pork, chicken, or turkey. However, keep in mind that they're low in fat. You must prepare them carefully with plenty of low temperatures and extra moisture while covering them up.

Do not cook beyond an internal temperature of 165F for the best results, and let it rest for 5-10 minutes after finishing the meal.

It can be served with everyday sides when roasted, or you can get creative. Make sure you brine or marinate to keep moisture.

☰ QUAIL

Butchering Quail

If you want a whole bird with the skin on it, you can do so. Many people choose to remove the skin, but keeping it can help keep the meat moist. The crispy skin is delicious as well. This process involves first removing the head, then dipping the body in boiling water to scald the feathers and skin. It is done for about 30 seconds, and after, the feathers will come off with gentle rubbing motions. Then, you can start processing the rest of the bird.

Rinse off the bird, bend the leg joints, and cut them off. Use kitchen shears to cut from the tail up either side of the spine, spatchcocking it. This will remove the backbone. Without the spine, be able to pull out the neck. Then, all the insides can be gently scooped out. Clean out the cavity and put the bird in the fridge or use it immediately. You'll have a whole bird that can be roasted and enjoyed.

If you want to harvest without skin, you can skip the scalding step and snip off the head and feet. While running water, get a finger underneath the skin at the neck and slowly peel it from the muscle. Then, cut the bird as if you were keeping the skin on and empty the cavity. Clean it up and prepare it for storage.

Storing Quail

Let the meat sit for 24 hours in the fridge or an ice chest overnight for tenderizing. You can also lightly brine it with a bit of salt to help preserve and flavor the meat. You can use freezer bags to freeze it with a vacuum seal.

Tips for Cooking Quail

Quail is very easy to overcook, which renders the meat dry and tough. It is cooked through when the meat is firm like a chicken breast, with clear juices.

The whole quail can be stuffed and cooked a little longer. Make sure the center is cooked thoroughly before serving.

☰ DUCK

Butchering Duck

Like other birds, you can choose to either skin the duck or scald them to pluck. It depends on if you want the skin to be kept to eat or not. With the skin, the bird will be juicier, and you can save the fat. However, ducks are harder to pluck than other birds.

To remove feathers, scald and pluck.

To skin the bird, begin at the neck and cut under the skin. Slice through the skin underneath where you removed the head, then slice down the belly toward the tail. You should be able to pull the skin, separating with the knife. Work your way around the whole bird. For the wings, you can cut off the ends and skin the other joints. From there, it's time to disembowel the gut.

Cut around the vent without puncturing the bowels. Then starting at the belly, cut from the vent to the ribcage. Then you can get the bird. Remove feet and neck, slicing through ligaments between bones rather than cutting through the bone itself.

Clean out the bird, wash thoroughly, and chill. If you want to butcher further, you can cut down the spine to spatchcock the bird and separate it into quarters or eighths.

Storing Duck

Keep the meat in the fridge for 24 hours, soaking in brine. You can freeze after the 24-hour soak to have a much more tender bird. Dry well, then put the bird in freezer bags.

Tips for Cooking Duck

Duck is easier to crisp when using a whole bird.

Serve duck breast medium rare for best taste.

If serving whole, keep in mind that duck breasts have a thick layer of fat, which needs to render when cooking. You can score the skin with a criss-cross and cook skin-side down to melt fat away. If you don't score and prick the skin, you will have greasy meat.

Duck legs are salted overnight then cooked in duck fat to cook slowly to keep them soft.

☰ TURKEY

Butchering Turkey

Most of the time, people butcher hunted turkeys down to breasts, legs, and wings. It's not practical to often keep turkeys in the entire form, though you could cook it fresh from whole if you wanted to. Butchering a turkey is simple. If you've already cleaned the bird, you can remove the skin and start separating the pieces.

Begin at the breast, using a sharp, flexible blade to get through the meat and take as much as you can. Cut a bit of skin on the breast and tear it open. It will be tough, but you will reveal the breast in doing so. Do this on both sides to expose the whole breast.

Start on the breastbone with a sharp, flexible blade and follow the bone as closely as possible as you work the meat free. Don't puncture the crop while doing so. Separate the crop from the breast and pull it away, so it doesn't puncture and taint the meat, then finish pulling the breast off. Do so on both sides.

Next, you remove the legs. The leg is already revealed due to skinning the breast. Put a blade in to cut the skin down the leg, all the way to the part where it becomes scaly. Pull it off of the leg, and you'll have a clean leg. At the base of the thigh, be able to see the end of the thigh. Cut carefully to separate the thigh from the body. Then, dislocate the joint, pull it free, and slice if necessary. The leg should come free. Chop the leg between the knee and ankle joint, right where the scales begin. You can keep the spurs if you want. Put a knife to cut the ligaments in the joint, twist, and cut any remaining connective tissue. Do this on both ends.

If you want to keep the wings too, you can pop out the wing joint, pushing it from the body, then cut the wing off. It can be sectioned into the drumette and the wingette, at which point you can start plucking and skinning. This is a lot of work, so weigh if you're interested in doing so.

Storing Turkey

When broken down, the turkey should be vacuum-sealed to keep the meat tasting fresh for a year. Keeping it in pieces is often easier than keeping it whole.

Tips for Cooking Turkey

The leg meat can be tender if cooked well. Be careful not to overcook it or it will dry out.

Wings and drumsticks do well in the crockpot.

The gizzard, liver, and heart can be kept and enjoyed.

Consider saving the bones for stock.

GEESE

Butchering Geese

While you could pluck the goose, it's easier to skin them and be done with it. They have a very thick down that can be difficult to separate. If you want to scald them, you can, adding a bit of dish soap to the water to help penetrate the feathers.

You could leave the goose whole, or you could break it up into several pieces.

Remove the goose's head and neck, reserving the neck for use later.

Legs can be removed by cutting along the leg and thigh, following the body's natural shape. Cut all the way, then dislocate the thigh joint and cut the rest of the flesh, holding it in place. Make a slit around where the ligament connects to the drumstick, all the way around. Then use the back of a knife to break the joint just above where the leg meets the ankle and pull. You'll have a clean bone and remove the sinew. Do this on both sides.

Wings can be cut off straight between the joints and cook with the legs.

Remove the wishbone so you can remove the breast. Make an incision on either side of the wishbone, twist, and pull. Then, you can remove the breasts. Cut toward the breastbone at an angle following the bone to free the breast and the bottom wing joint. Do this on both sides, and you've preserved much of the meat.

You can further trim the breast, removing the wing. Then, trim the fat off the breast. Remove any sinew as well.

Storing Geese

Goose can be stored frozen and sealed in a vacuum seal.

Tips for Cooking Geese

Goose is very greasy if you're not careful. Score the fat before cooking to help it render well.

The legs and wings are typically cooked in a confit.

BULLFROG

Butchering Bullfrog

Bullfrogs are butchered during the field dressing process. Remember that to do so, you remove the feet, slice skin around the frogs' waist, then pull the skin off like pants. You can then use shears to chop off the leg.

Storing Bullfrog

Freeze legs in 1-lb packs in vacuum-sealed bags.

Tips for Cooking Bullfrog

Bullfrog should be cooked after soaking it in milk to mellow out the flavor. After soaking them, they can be treated like chicken wings.

SNAPPING TURTLES

Butchering Snapping Turtle

After you've cleaned and skinned a snapping turtle (revisit the field dressing guide to doing so), you can then butcher it up. Doing so is easy. Begin by quartering the limbs. Then, cut off the neck and tail.

Use a knife to cut down the backstrap, trimming them as you go. Remove damaged, fat, or sinew. Then, you can store it in pieces.

Storing Snapping Turtle

To store meat, soak overnight in saltwater first. Then, you can use it or freeze it in vacuum-sealed bags.

Tips for Cooking Snapping Turtle

Snapping turtles can be pressure-cooked to keep the meat tender.

If you don't pressure cook the turtle, consider simmering it to tenderize it. Turtle meat can be tough if not cooked well. It may also be fried.

SECRET RECIPES FOR DELICIOUSNESS

SQUIRREL RECIPES

DRUNKEN SQUIRREL AND PUMPKIN DUMPLINGS

Time: 2 hours 45 minutes
Servings: 4

Ingredients

For the dumplings:

- Cooked pureed squash (1 cup)
- Flour (2 3/4 cups)
- Nutmeg (1/4 tsp, ground)
- Eggs (2, beaten lightly)
- Ricotta cheese (1 cup)

- Parmesan cheese (1/4 cup)
- Salt (a pinch)
- Butter (3 Tbsp.)

For the squirrel:
- Butter (3 Tbsp.)
- Squirrel thighs (2 lbs)
- Salt to taste
- Vermouth (1 cup)
- Bay leaves 6
- Squirrel stock (1/2 cup; can substitute chicken stock if you don't have any)

For the veggies:
- Butter (2 Tbsp.)
- Onion (1, sliced)
- Garlic (2 cloves, thin sliced)
- Kale (1 lb., chopped)
- Pecans (1/2 cup)
- Salt and pepper to taste

Instructions

1. Prepare the squirrel. Set the oven to 325F and use cast iron or other ovenproof pans, melt butter, and browning squirrel legs. They should be nicely browned.

2. When browned, toss in the vermouth to deglaze the pan. Don't forget to scrape the brown parts stuck to the pan. Toss in the stock and bay leaves, put a cover

on the pot, and cook in the oven for 2 hours until the meat is tender but not entirely falling off the bone.

3. Prepare the dumplings next. Begin by mixing the ricotta, squash puree, eggs, and parmesan into a bowl. Toss with salt and nutmeg. Then, start adding flour 1 cup at a time. You may need extra to get a nice dough.

4. Prepare a big pot of boiling water. Then, toss in some salt.

5. Roll the dough into a long log that's about as thick as a finger. Then make pieces roughly 1/4 inch thick. Wipe the knife as necessary.

6. Place out a baking sheet with flour, then use it to roll each piece of dough into round balls. Flour is key to avoiding sticking.

7. Cook the dumplings in the water in batches, waiting for the dumplings to float and waiting another minute. Take out the dumplings and leave them on an oiled baking sheet.

8. When the squirrel is done cooking, take it to the stovetop. Take another large pan with 3 Tbsp. Butter on medium-high. Put the dumplings in a single layer. Let them sear for a minute and a half to two minutes, letting them brown. Then toss the pan and mix them up for another few minutes to sear more. Take them out, put them in a bowl, and put the bowl in the oven (which should be off and still warm.)

9. Add more butter to the pan if there isn't much left in there. Then, toss in the onions and let them cook for 6-8 minutes. Stir regularly. Then add in the kale, pecans, and garlic, sauteeing for a few minutes to coat

everything. Drop the heat down and cover the pan until the kale is wilted.

10. Serve warm and enjoy.

PAPRIKA SQUIRREL STEW

Time: 2 hours, 20 minutes
Servings: 8

Ingredients

- Squirrel (3 whole, cut into serving pieces)
- Salt to taste
- Flour to prevent sticking
- Olive oil (⅓ cup)
- Onions (2 cups, sliced)
- Garlic (3 cloves, minced)
- Tomato paste (1 Tbsp.)
- White wine (1 cup)
- Cider vinegar (1/4 cup)
- Oregano (1 tsp)
- Red pepper flakes (1/2 tsp)
- Paprika (1 Tbsp.)
- Tomatoes (2-3 cups, whole peeled, torn up)
- Smoked sausage (1 lb., kielbasa works well)
- Greens (1 lb., kale, chard, etc.)
- Pepper to taste

Instructions

1. Make sure all pieces of squirrel are butchered down into pieces. Then, salt and coat with a bit of flour. Use some olive oil in a Dutch oven on medium-high heat. Cook the squirrel in single-layer batches without over-crowding the pot. As you do, move browned pieces to the side while finishing the rest.

2. When all pieces are browned and set aside, saute the onion until it browns on the edges. Then, cook in the garlic for another minute. Mix in tomato paste and let it cook for 3 minutes with regular stirring.

3. Toss in white wine, vinegar, and 1 quart of water. Mix the oregano, red pepper, and paprika in. Then mix in the tomatoes and finally, the squirrel. Combine well and simmer it. Cook until the squirrel falls off the bone, roughly 90 minutes. Pull out the squirrel to remove all bones, then toss the meat back into the pot. Salt to taste.

4. Mix in the sausage and greens for another 10 minutes until the greens are done. Mix in salt and pepper if necessary and vinegar to taste and enjoy.

≡ **RABBIT RECIPES**

RABBIT CURRY

Time: 1 hour
Servings: 4

Ingredients

- Vegetable oil (1/4 cup)
- Rabbit meat (2 lbs., removed from the bone and cut in chunks)
- Salt (to taste)
- Yellow onion (2 cups, sliced)
- Ginger (2 Tbsp., minced)
- Garlic (2 Tbsp. minced)
- Tomato puree (1 can, 14 oz.)
- Greek yogurt (1 cup)
- Water (2 cups)
- Bay leaves (2)
- Turmeric (1 tsp)
- Curry powder (2 Tbsp.)
- Garam masala (1 Tbsp.)
- Cilantro (1/4 cup, chopped)

Instructions

1. War oil in a large pot on medium-high. Dry the rabbit with a paper towel, then saute until browned. As the meat cooks, season with salt. When they're brown, remove them into a bowl and set them aside.

2. Toss in the onions to the pan and allow them to saute until the edges turn brown. Then, toss in garlic and ginger until fragrant, another minute.

3. Toss the meat back into the pan alongside the tomato, bay leaves, curry powder, turmeric, and water. Mix in the yogurt gently, simmering. Then salt to taste before simmering for 30 minutes.

4. Finish up with garam masala and cilantro, then serve over rice.

ORANGE RABBIT

Time: 2 hours 30 minutes
Servings: 6

Ingredients

- Olive oil (2 Tbsp.)
- Garlic (4 cloves)
- Salt (1 Tbsp.)
- Orange juice (1 cup)
- Rabbit (6 pieces, roughly 2.5 lbs.)
- Red onion (2, thinly sliced)
- Lemon juice (1 cup)

Instructions

1. Combine the oil, garlic, orange juice, and salt in a blender until the garlic is finely minced. Then, put the rabbit into a bowl or bag that can be sealed and marinate it in the mixture for an hour.

2. Preheat the oven to 400 degrees F. Then, move the rabbit to a casserole dish. Cover it up with foil and cook for 15 minutes, then drop the temperature down to 325 F and roast for an hour.

3. Slice up the onion and marinate in lemon juice and salt.

4. Serve the rabbit on a bed of lettuce, topped with the marinated onion slices. Enjoy!

☰ GROUSE RECIPES

SAUTEED GROUSE AND PEACH-BALSAMIC SAUCE

Time: 50 minutes
Servings: 4

Ingredients

- Butter (2 Tbsp.)
- Garlic (2 cloves)
- Grouse (2 birds, cut into quarters)
- White wine (1 cup)
- Chicken stock (1/4 cup)
- Tarragon (2 tsp)
- Peach jam (1/2 cup)
- Balsamic vinegar (1 tsp)

Instructions

1. In a large skillet, melt the butter on low, mixing in the garlic. Let it bubble gently for 10 minutes to infuse the garlic into the butter fully. Pull out the garlic and set it aside.

2. Raise the heat to medium-high, then brown the grouse in the butter. It should brown for about 3 minutes per side until golden. Then remove the grouse and set it aside.

3. When the grouse is ready, pour in white wine into the skillet, simmering for 20 seconds, and deglaze the pan. Then, mix in the chicken stock, jam, and

tarragon. Let it simmer for 5 minutes on medium-low. Mix in the vinegar and let cook for another 2 minutes.

4. Put the grouse back in the pan with the sauce and finish cooking, another 3-5 minutes.

ROAST GROUSE

Time: 25 minutes
Servings: 2

Ingredients

- Whole grouse (2)
- Butter (10 grams)
- Juniper berries (1 tsp., crushed)
- Thyme (4 sprigs)
- Salt and pepper to taste
- Streaky bacon (4 rashers)

Instructions

1. Set the oven to 400F. Then, season the birds with salt and pepper on the inside and out. Put the berries into the cavities, then place a sprig of thyme underneath each leg. Place two pieces of bacon over the breast of each grouse.

2. Warm butter (or duck fat if you have it) in an oven-proof pan. Sear the birds' backs, then each side until golden brown. Turn them on their backs.

3. Roast for 15-20 minutes, depending on their size. Then let them rest for 5 minutes before serving.

≡ PARTRIDGE RECIPES

HERBY ROAST PARTRIDGE

Time: 45 minutes
Servings: 4

Ingredients

- Partridges (4, young and plump)
- Thyme (6 sprigs)
- Juniper berries (12)
- Butter (100g)
- Bacon (8 thin rashers)
- Pears (2)
- Lemon juice (a splash)
- White bread (4 slices)
- Rowan or quince jelly (2 Tbsp.)
- Vermouth (1 glass)

Instructions

1. Make sure all birds are feather-free while the oven preheats to 425F.
2. Remove the leaves from the thyme sprigs, then crush them with the juniper berries, butter, and salt and pepper (to taste) with a mortar and pestle. Keep 1 Tbsp. Aside and use the rest to spread over the birds, focusing on the breasts.

3. Put bacon on a chopping board and stretch them out to thin them without breaking them. Then wrap them over the birds, putting them in a roasting tin.

4. Slice the pears, mixing with a splash of lemon juice. Then, cook in the Tbsp. of herby butter. When they'repale gold, move them to the roasting tin with thepartridges. Roast for 20 minutes, then peel the baconoff if it has become crisp. If the birds aren't done, cook for another 10 minutes.

5. Take the bread and cut it into little squares. Warm a bit of butter in the pan used for the pears. Then, fry until the bread becomes crisp and drain well on a paper towel.

6. Pull the tin out of the oven and set birds on fried bread. Place bacon and pear beside them. Put the roasting pan over a medium temperature and mix in the jelly to melt, then add the wine to deglaze the pan. Boil, then use as a gravy.

PARTRIDGE BAKED BEANS

Time: 10 hours
Servings: 8

Ingredients

- Dried great northern beans (2 cups)
- Salt pork (2 oz., cubed in 1 inch" pieces)
- Dried mustard (1tsp)
- Dark brown sugar (1/2 cup)
- Molasses (1/2 cup)

- Ketchup (2 Tbsp.)
- Salt and pepper
- Partridge (1 whole bird, cut in 6-8 pieces)
- Chicken stock (2 cups)

Instructions

1. Put the beans in a big casserole dish to soak in coldwater for 4 hours overnight. Drain them and thenput the beans back in the casserole dish with 3cups of water.

2. Set the oven to 300 degrees F. Put in the pork, mustard, onions, brown sugar, ketchup, and molasses. Season with salt and pepper to taste. Then, bake until beans are tender, up to 5 hours. If they dry out, add more water as necessary.

3. Put partridge in a medium pot with the stock. Cover and cook on medium until the meat falls off the bones, roughly 50-60 minutes. Remove the bones.

4. Combine the partridge with the stock and beans together right before serving.

≡ **DOVE RECIPES**

TERIYAKI DOVE

Time: 1 hour, 30 minutes
Servings: 4

Ingredients

- Sake (1/4 cup)
- Mirin (1/4 cup)
- Rice vinegar (2 Tbsp.)
- Soy sauce (3 Tbsp.)
- Sugar (2 tsp)
- Corn starch - (1/2 tsp to thicken—can be omitted if you don't want a thick sauce.)
- Doves (12)
- Vegetable oil (3 Tbsp.)
- Sesame oil
- Sesame seeds for garnish

Instructions

1. Combine the sake, mirin, soy sauce, and sugar in a pot, warming until the sugar dissolves. Then, turn the heat off and let it cool. When cool, bathe the birds in the marinade, breast down for an hour.
2. Put the marinade in a pot and boil to a syrup, or thicken with cornstarch and water. Add vinegar to taste.

3. Heat your grill well, scraping the grates and closing the lids. Use some vegetable oil on a paper towel and a pair of tongs to grease the grill grates, then lightly coat the birds with sesame oil. Place them breast up on the grill with the lid closed for 4 minutes.

4. Open the lid and slather the doves with the reduced marinade. Turn them onto their sides to paint the bottom as well. Grill with the cover opens for another 2 minutes to grill the sides as well.

5. Turn the bird's breast down and paint the bottom with the marinade. Grill another 2-3 minutes with the cover open to brown the skin.

6. Take them off from the heat, coat with marinade sauce, and let cool for 5 minutes. Serve sprinkled with sesame seeds.

DOVE AND CORNBREAD CASSEROLE

Time: 1 hour 30 minutes
Servings: 4

Ingredients

- Dove breast (8)
- Celery (1/2 cup, chopped)
- Green onion (1/4 cup, sliced)
- Parsley (2 Tbsp., fresh)
- Butter (1/4 cup)
- Cornbread stuffing mix (3 cups)
- Chicken broth (1 cup)
- Marjoram leaves (1/2 tsp)

- Salt (1/2 tsp)
- Pepper ($\frac{1}{8}$ tsp)

Instructions

1. Set the oven to 350F and grease a casserole dish.
2. In a large pan, saute the onion, celery, and parsley in butter on medium heat. They should become tender.
3. Toss in everything but the dove. Mix well until thoroughly moist. Put half of the stuffing mix in the casserole dish. Then, place the dove breasts over the stuffing. Cover entirely with the rest of the stuffing.
4. Bake without a cover for about an hour until the dove is tender.

☰ PHEASANT RECIPES

PHEASANT PICCATA

Time: 25 minutes
Servings: 5

Ingredients

- Pheasant breasts (10)
- Salt (1 tsp)
- Pepper (1 tsp)
- Flour (⅓ cup)
- Unsalted butter (3 Tbsp.)
- Olive oil (3 Tbsp.)
- Chicken broth (1/2 cup)
- White wine (1/2 cup or AS MUCH AS DESIRE! LOL!)
- Capers (2 Tbsp.)
- Lemon juice (2 Tbsp.)
- Lemon (1, sliced)

Instructions

1. Season breasts with salt and pepper. Warm 2 Tbsp. Butter and 2 Tbsp. Olive oil over medium heat.

2. When the butter has melted and mixed with oil, dredge each breast in flour for a light coating. Then saute for 3-4 minutes on each side until proper internal temperature has been reached (165 F). Cook in two batches to prevent overcrowding if necessary,

keeping the first batch warm in foil while cooking the second batch.

3. When all breasts are cooked, use chicken broth, wine, remaining butter, lemon, and capers to the pan. Mix well to deglaze the bottom of the skillet, scraping well, and simmer for 3 minutes.

4. Serve breasts with a spoonful of buttery lemon sauce drizzled over, with a side of pasta or potatoes.

TANGERINE ROASTED PHEASANT

Time: 2 hours
Servings: 4

Ingredients

- Garlic (1 clove)
- Salt
- Tangerine juice (fresh squeezed, from 2 tangerines)
- Tangerine zest (1 ½ tsp)
- Tangerine (1, halved)
- Tarragon (1 tsp, dried)
- Olive oil (2 Tbsp.)
- Pepper (to taste)
- Carrots (2, halved and cut into 2-inch pieces)
- Potatoes (1/2 lb, quartered)
- Plum tomatoes (4, ripe, halved, and seeded)
- Pheasant (2 1/2 lb)
- Tarragon (2 sprigs)
- Tart apple (1/2, cored and cut)
- Shallots (2, peeled and halved)

- Sage (3-4 sprigs)
- Turkey bacon (3 slices)
- Chicken broth (⅛ cup)

Instructions

1. Set the oven to 350 F. Mince garlic and mix with salt in a bowl. Mix in the tangerine juice and zest, olive oil, tarragon, and pepper. Set mixture aside.

2. Blanch the potato and carrot for 7 minutes. Then, drain well and set aside in a bowl with tomatoes.

3. Loosen the skin of the pheasants gently, placing a sprig of tarragon on each side. Gently put the skin back in place. Squeeze the tangerine into the cavity, sprinkling in salt and pepper. Mix in the shallots, apple, and sage into the cavity, and tie the legs with twine.

4. Put veggies in a roasting pan, tossing with the garlic-tangerine mix. Put the pheasant atop veggies, breast up, then brush with some of the tangerine oil. Spread the three pieces of bacon over the breast and pour broth at the bottom of the pan.

5. Roast for an hour, basting every 20 minutes. Remove the bacon and roast another 20-30 minutes until done. Let rest for 10 minutes. Carve and serve.

☰ QUAIL RECIPES

TANDOORI QUAIL

Time: 45 minutes

Servings: 4

Ingredients

- Greek yogurt (1 cup plain)
- Lemon juice (2 Tbsp.)
- Lime juice (2 Tbsp.)
- Ginger (1 Tbsp., grated)
- Garlic (2 cloves, grated)
- Paprika (1 Tbsp.)
- Coriander (2 tsp)
- Cumin (2 tsp)
- Turmeric (1 tsp)
- Cilantro (3 Tbsp.)
- Quail (8, halved lengthwise)
- Salt and pepper
- Vegetable oil

Instructions

1. Mix yogurt, lemon and lime juice, ginger, garlic, cilantro, coriander, cumin, turmeric, 2 tsp salt, 1 Tbsp
   oil in a bowl. Combine well, then transfer to a large
   resealable bag. Toss in the quail and seal, pressing out
   air. Refrigerate overnight.

2. Pull out the quail and let it stand for 30 minutes to come to room temperature.

3. Light a grill, oil the grates. Season the quail with salt and pepper. Grill, turning once until meat is barely pink. Transfer to a platter and garnish with cilantro. Serve.

FRIED QUAIL

Time: 20 minutes
Servings: 4

Ingredients

- Quail (8, whole)
- Salt and pepper to taste
- Flour
- Peanut oil

Instructions

1. Rinse quail and pat it dry with paper towels.
2. Season the birds with salt and pepper on the inside and out.
3. Coat the quail in flour to coat thoroughly.
4. Heat 1 inch of oil in a cast-iron skillet to get it hot enough to fry.
5. Put quail in the oil and fry, turning until it's golden brown everywhere.
6. Pull the quail out and let it dry on a paper towel. Serve and enjoy.

≡ DUCK RECIPES

ROAST DUCK

Time: 2 hours
Servings: 4

Ingredients

- Ducks (2, go for fat ones)
- Kosher salt (1 Tbsp.)
- Lemon (1, cut in half)
- Rosemary, parsley, or thyme (4 sprigs)

Instructions

1. Set the oven to 325F. Use a needle to prick the skin all over the duck skin, careful not to pierce the meat to release the fat. Don't forget to prick the back and sides.
2. Rub cut lemon all over the ducks, then stick. of the lemon in each cavity.
3. Salt the birds liberally, then stuff with the herbs. Let sit at room temperature for 30 minutes.
4. Roast the ducks in a large cast-iron pan, or another ovenproof pan. Start checking at 40 minutes. It could take up to 90 minutes for a large or store-bought duck, depending on size. Pull the duck out and baste it.
5. Boost temperature to 450F. When preheated, put the birds back in the oven. Crisp the skin for 15-20 minutes or until crisp.
6. Let birds rest for 5-10 minutes before serving.

DUCK RAGU

Time: 2 hours 50 minutes
Servings: 4

Ingredients

- Duck legs (2 large)
- Carrot (1, chopped finely)
- Onion (1, chopped finely)
- Celery (1 stalk, chopped finely)
- Orange zest (. orange peel worth)
- Cinnamon (1 tsp)
- Pureed tomato (1 cup)
- Tomato paste (1 Tbsp.)
- White wine (⅔ cup or AS MUCH AS DESIRE! LOL.)
- Chicken stock (5 cups)
- Salt and pepper to taste
- Bay leaf (1)
- Olive oil (2 Tbsp.)
- Pappardelle pasta (14 oz)
- Parmesan cheese to taste

Instructions

1. Season the duck legs with salt and pepper. Then, rub it with ½ tsp cinnamon. Sear the legs in a large pan using a bit of olive oil for 7-8 minutes per side until they're brown. Set them aside.

2. Pour 1 Tbsp. Olive oil into the pan, then saute the carrot, onion, celery, orange zest, bay leaf, and the remainder of the cinnamon. Let it saute for 10 minutes, stirring regularly.

3. Put in the duck, then mix with the wine. Reduce the wine by 50%, then add the juice, pureed tomato, and tomato paste. Stir well, then mix in the stock. Simmer uncovered for 2 hours. If the sauce reduces too much, add more stock.

4. Turn the sauce off and pull out the duck. Let the duck cool for 10 minutes on a cutting board, then shred the meat. Chop, then toss back into the sauce.

5. Prepare the pasta according to instructions, then serve.

TURKEY RECIPES

GRILLED TURKEY BITES

Time: 2 hours 10 minutes
Servings: 6

Ingredients

- Bacon (1 lb, thick-cut)
- Turkey breast (1-1/2 breast, cubed into 1 ½ " pieces)
- Jalapenos (3, sliced in coins)
- Olive oil (1/4 cup.)
- White vinegar (2 Tbsp.)
- Worcestershire sauce (2 Tbsp.)
- Pepper (1/2 tsp)
- Garlic (2 cloves, minced)
- Salt (1 tsp)
- Brown sugar (1 Tbsp.)

Instructions

1. Mix vinegar, worcestershire sauce, pepper, salt, garlic cloves, and sugar together. Then, marinate the turkey in the mixture for 2 hours.
2. Cut bacon strips in half.
3. Put one jalapeno slice in the center of each piece of bacon and then one cube of turkey on top of the jalapeno. Wrap well, then pin together with a toothpick. Repeat this for all the turkey.
4. Put the grill on medium heat (350 degrees). Put rolls on the sides and cook slowly, turning regularly. Turkey

should be done when bacon is fully cooked. Let it rest for 5 minutes and serve.

☰ TURKEY FRIED RICE

Time: 30 minutes
Servings: 4

Ingredients

- Vegetable oil (6 tsp)
- Eggs (2)
- Turkey breast (1 cup, diced)
- Bell pepper (1, chopped)
- Onion (1, chopped)
- Soy sauce (to taste)
- Carrots (2, julienned)
- Cooked rice (2 cups, preferably a day old)
- Broccoli (1 cup, florets)

Instructions

1. Heat a wok with 2 tsp oil. Toss in the veggies and saute until they are tender-crisp.
2. Remove the veggies and set them aside.
3. Add 2 more tsp oil and scramble eggs. Remove the eggs when set and set aside.
4. Toss in the remainder of the oil and cook the turkey breast until done roughly 10 minutes—season to taste with soy sauce. Then toss the veggies and eggs into the wok. Mix well, then toss in the rice and any extra soy sauce if desired. Mix well and serve hot.

☰ GOOSE RECIPES

BBQ PULLED GOOSE

Time: 6 hours
Servings: 8

Ingredients

- Goose breast (2 lb., boneless and skinless)
- Butter (2 Tbsp.)
- Onion (1, chopped)
- Garlic (3 cloves, crushed)
- Worcestershire sauce (1/4 cup)
- Chicken stock (2-4 cups as needed)
- Barbecue sauce (to taste)

Instructions

1. Warm butter in a skillet, then brown breast on all sides over medium heat.
2. Move the meat to a slow cooker. Toss in the garlic, onion, Worcestershire sauce, and enough stock that will cover the meat.
3. Simmer for 6-8 hours on low until the meat shreds readily with a fork.
4. Remove the meat and shred.
5. Discard the liquid in the slow cooker. Mix the shredded meat in with your favorite BBQ sauce. Let it warm up and serve on buns.

GOOSE TACOS

Time: 2 hours, 30 minutes
Servings: 4

Ingredients

- Goose breasts (2 large)
- Canola oil (2 Tbsp.)
- Soy sauce (1/2 cup)
- Lager beer (⅓ cup)
- Black pepper (1 tsp)
- Cayenne powder (1 tsp)
- Garlic powder (1 tsp)

Instructions

1. Butterfly the breasts, then pound them out to a thickness of . inch. Mix soy sauce, beer, and seasonings together, then marinate the duck for 2 hours, up to overnight.

2. When ready to cook, pull the breasts out, dry them off, and lightly oil them. Sear them down on a heavy frying pan, and place a heavyweight or another flat top pan on top of the meat to press it flat while searing. Do this for 3 minutes.

3. Flip the meat and press another 1-3 minutes until done.

4. Remove the meat and rest it for a few minutes. Then, cut thinly against the grain into taco-sized bits. Serve with tortillas and toppings of choice.

BULLFROG RECIPE

LOUISIANA FROG LEGS

Time: 2 hours 30 minutes
Servings: 5-8

Ingredients

- Frog legs (20-40)
- Peanut oil
- Buttermilk (1 qt)
- Eggs (2)
- Dijon mustard (4 Tbsp.)
- White flour (3 cups)
- Cornmeal (1 cup)
- Salt and pepper to taste
- Cajun seasoning to taste

Instructions

1. Soak frog legs in buttermilk for an hour. Then, take them out and pat dry.
2. Put the legs in a dry bowl and season with salt and pepper, cajun seasoning, and any hot sauce or worcestershire sauce you may want. Marinate another 30 minutes in the fridge.
3. Pull legs from the fridge and let them drip on a baking rack.
4. Heat 1 inch of peanut oil in a fryer until 375 degrees.

5. Make an egg wash, beating eggs with a splash of water or beer. Then, add in cajun seasoning, garlic powder, salt and pepper, mustard, hot sauce, and worcester-shire sauce.

6. Mix two cups of flour and cornmeal in another bowl. Season to taste.

7. Dredge each frog leg in the last of the plain flour, then dip in egg wash, and in seasoned flour/cornmeal mix. Repeat until all legs are ready to fry.

8. Fry for 3 minutes on each side until golden. Enjoy!

☰ SNAPPING TURTLE RECIPE

CREOLE TURTLE SOUP

Time: 3 hours 30 minutes
Servings: 6-8

Ingredients

- Turtle meat (11/2 lb, boneless or 2 ½ lb bone-in)
- Bay leaves (4)
- Salt
- Flour (1 cup)
- Butter (8 Tbsp.)
- Celery (2 stalks, minced)
- Onion (1 ½ cups, minced)
- Bell pepper (1, green, minced)
- Garlic (4 cloves, minced)
- Crushed tomatoes (1 18oz. can)
- Paprika (1 Tbsp.)
- Worcestershire sauce (3 Tbsp.)
- Sherry (1/2 cup)
- Parsley (⅓ cup, chopped)
- Hard-Boiled eggs (2, chopped)
- Lemon zest
- Pepper to taste
- Lemon juice (2 Tbsp.)

Instructions

1. Make turtle stock. Put meat in a pot with 8 cups of water, bay leaves, and 1 Tbsp. Salt. Boil and skim the scum. Let simmer until meat is falling off bones, 2-3 hours.

2. Remove meat and pull off bones, then chop. Strain broth, then put it in a pot over low.

3. Take a dutch oven and melt the butter on medium-high. Then, mix in flour to make a roux. It will take 15 minutes.

4. Toss in green pepper, celery, and onion, then cook for 5 minutes. Then, mix in the garlic for another minute. Toss in the chopped turtle meat and combine well.

5. Mix in turtle stock, 1 cup at a time, until the consistency of gravy.

6. Mix in tomatoes, worcestershire sauce, paprika, and cayenne pepper. It should be thinner than gravy.

7. Simmer for 15 minutes until veggies are soft.

8. Top with the sherry, some lemon zest, and the egg. Then, combine well. Serve, using salt, pepper, and lemon juice to taste.

FINAL WORDS

And that, my friend, brings us to the end of this guide. It has covered a wide range of topics on some of the most essential information in hunting small game. From locating and tracking small game to field dressing, skinning, and preparing the food to enjoy, all the information is there for you to use. Whether you're a new hunter or interested, the information provided iscrucial if you want to be successful. And now, you're ready! You've got all the working knowledge to prepare yourself for hunting, prepping, and eating your meat. You are one step closer to self-sufficiency, and you've learned valuable life skills that will take you far. Hunting is one of the most incredible ways to connect to nature, recognizing the beautiful bounties left behind for you, and now, you can enjoy them yourself. Good luck on your hunting journey, and remember this: hunting is about respect. It is about respect for nature, respect for the animal whose meat you will enjoy, and respect for yourself.

HUNTING FOR GREATNESS COMMUNITY!

COME DISCOVER THE MOST VALUABLE
HUNTING COMMUNITY!

www.facebook.com/groups/www.huntingsecrets

A Special Gift To Our Readers!

Included with your purchase of this book is our Field Dressing Starters Guide. This guide will prepare you with some essential critical tips not to forget when you start field dressing small game. It has a secret golden nugget at the end, too!

www.patgatz.com

* 9 7 8 1 7 7 7 8 7 7 9 2 7 *